About the Author

From a young age I have loved to travel. This stems from having grown up in East Africa and flying back and forth to the UK as an unaccompanied minor with a passport slung around my neck.

These early experiences led my young family and I in 2008 to embark on an epic overland trip in a Land Rover from Sweden to Malawi via Iran and Syria.

Now a grown-up and working as a European Sales Manager, I have the chance to travel across most of Europe visiting Golf courses and Football pitches alike in the hope to sell something to them, usually over a glass or two of wine.

Turf Travels

Richard Poskitt

FIRST EDITION: December 2020

The Events and conversations in this book have been set down to the best of the author's ability, although some names and details have been changed to protect the privacy of individuals

Cover design by Lina Poskitt

ISBN: 9798558037265

For Lina, Tuvalie, Oliver and Anton

Introduction

This book takes place during the year 2019, and the first few months of 2020.

The context is my memoirs of travelling around Europe as a sales manager for a fertiliser company. Having such a role, I feel fortunate to see, experience, and delve into the world of business travel. It all changed when the Corona Virus Pandemic took its hold of the world of cross border travel in 2020 so this is my life before then.

I often wander the streets of a visiting city or town. I suppose I am true to the definition of *Dromomania*. The desire or urge to walk and travel. The only thing for me is it tends to involve drinks and good food.

In this book, I have named many of the places I have visited, not to review them, even though I have, but to give you the best and the worst with the funny little moments along the way that have made them special for me. Some of my customers are mentioned, and even competitors too. It is a small world in the sales of sports-turf products and not mentioning these people would lose the backbone of this story.

People lucky enough to work from wherever they happen to be often are regarded as travelling nomads, or in my industry, Turf Travellers. Not based in one spot or desk, but popping up a laptop and logging in from anywhere. There are a number of such "Turf Travel Nomads" mentioned in this book. It takes a certain amount of discipline to accomplish it well. I claim to be on no such pedestal. I find it hard to work on aeroplanes, trains and cars. But give me a quiet bar or cafe, and I can work forever. Observing my surroundings gives me a sense of being a part of the world and not missing out.

With the current of situation of the Pandemic, I do feel I am missing out. I miss travel, I miss meeting different people, and I miss the countries I visit frequently. But maybe it gives us all time to reflect on how we travel. I know that I have taken for granted many times the freedom of just booking a trip to meet clients when the reason for going can easily be done on a video conference call.

There is still a need to have face-to-face meetings. It is a must, but maybe these meetings will be different in the future, more intense perhaps, or longer a time allocated to them. At the time of writing this, the world is currently returning to a lockdown state with the second wave of the virus infections increasing across Europe. There is no sight of any responsible travel for the moment. It makes me sad. But my heart goes out to those affected.

I have often been asked if the constant travel, living in different hotels, and experiencing other cultures gives me pleasure or makes me happy. I certainly wake up happy each morning in the sense that thinks that I have one of the best jobs in the world. But the pleasure of travel is different from the happiness I get out of meeting new people and establishing relationships, both with my customers, but with the countries I visit. As Dr Lustig once said. "Pleasure is short-lived, and happiness is long-lived".

So in reading about my manic year and a bit of travel on more than 80 flights and scores of hotels, I hope you have pleasure in reading, but I wish more that it makes you smile and happy in the knowledge that there is someone out there, me, falling over every step of the way.

Contents

23.Lisbon

24.Tallinn Estonia

25.UK

26.Prague Czech Republic

27.Linz Austria

28.Birmingham UK

29.UK, Portugal, and Bulgaria

30.Italy and Slovenia

31.Almaria Spain

32.Iceland

33.Oslo Norway

34.UK 2020

35.Prague Czech Republic

36.Galway Ireland

37.Oslo Norway

38.Iceland

1. Lisbon Portugal January 2019

For the past four years the first trip of my working year has always been a few days conference in Southern Europe with a grass seed supplier. This is one of the very few events when our fellow distributors, and so competitors, get together for some sun, gin, and tonic. We talk about the seed market for a few hours of the two-day gathering with the rest of the time is spent listening to all the gossip of the sports turf industry in which we work.

I look forward to this trip very much. It gives a break from the depressing January weather in the UK. The Sales Manager always pops in some sort of cultural event or excursion surrounding the country or city we are visiting. Mostly this has been very interesting on the trips I have attended. The only one I can remember was a little odd was the Nigel Mansell Museum in Jersey. The displays of his amazing motorsport career are brilliant. The audio guide with Nigel, himself, guiding you around is a little hard going.

I have been on the BA jet from Gatwick to Jersey with him onboard on one occasion. I walked down the jetty just behind him. But being British shy, I did not ask him for a selfie or even an autograph. You are just going to have to believe me.

Anyway, I digress. This year the grass-seed gathering is to be Lisbon. A city I have not been before, so I am particularly looking forward to it. In preparation I looked up a few places in the city one must visit, the port, the statue to the explorers of the sea, and the cherry shots you can pick up on almost every street corner. I was also interested in a visit to the Elevador de Santa Justa, an elevator once driven by steam, and designed by Raoul Mesnier du Ponsard. Raoul worked with Eiffel on his tower. Although now converted to electricity, the elevator still brings in the crowds. It would be a brilliant trip.

The itinerary arrived in my inbox, and I did click right to it. We were to fly from Luton to Lisbon direct. It meant that I would have to travel more on a train within the UK than on the flight to Portugal, but no matter. It is supposed to be the most sun-kissed city in Europe, and that is all that counts in January.

On the plane, I sit next to a colleague of mine, Ian, who had won a sales competition to sell the most grass seed the prior year. Also on our row was the Financial Director of the company taking us there. He was entirely new and had not attended any of these events before. So naturally, he offered to buy drinks and some sort of food substance on the flight. We accepted his offer, twice.

I suggest that we have a packet of cheese crackers that I had only ever seen on this particular orange airline. "The Agronomist" (whom I shall introduce at a later stage) and I devoured several "Grate Britain Cheddar Crackers" together with a few wines on a trip back from Spain the previous December. They are unbelievably delicious.

Anyway, they did not have any onboard, so we had a Tapas selection instead, with wine.

Did I mention that Lisbon is known for its sun? Well, it was raining for our entire stay, and I shall not say anything more on the matter.

The hotel, a Tivoli variant, is friendly with spacious rooms and bright white extra large fluffy towels. A mark of a quality hotel by my book. Unfortunately, the hotel's location is a little out of the city for the ease of walking to the places I want to visit. Still, it has a rooftop bar with varying degrees of coloured lighting, and a good view of one of the river bridges. Drinks flowed, and the catching up with the group continued over a good set-menu dinner in the hotel restaurant.

I decide to get a sort of early night as the conference was starting at 9 am. I wanted to be fresh for it as it was the only bit of work-related time on the trip, and I did not wish to be hungover for this. Quite often on work trips salespeople especially go a little overboard on the first night and then suffer for the remainder of the trip. This act ruins it. I believe in settling down. Get to know the new surroundings and then you can, with the confidence of finding your way back to your room, go and enjoy yourself.

Waking up at 7 am, I go for the usual ritual of locating coffee. I do like an almost instant coffee, and the room came with a Nespresso machine to my delight. With the jug filled almost to the top —an almost impossibility due to the angle of the tap and the size of the washbasin. I slip in a coffee capsule and go to the toilet to read the news.

Halfway through the second article, some noise in the background was not quite right. Water dripping onto soft cloth. It was coming from my bedroom.

Shit!

The Nespresso machine was filling up the micro espresso cup with almost a litre of water. Having a slight panic, I quickly finished what I was doing. I discover on returning to the bedroom very diluted coffee everywhere over the tabletop and a flow of constant dripping onto the cream coloured carpet. I looked for something to deal with the mess. No tissues and the toilet roll was empty, and I had not located the spare yet. There was only one solution for it. I used one of the lovely fluffy white towels that festooned my bathroom and cleaned up the mess. I then made another coffee without moving from the machine and finally woke up.

The conference is always a fun one. There is banter, there are price increases, and there are still some dirty jokes made by a Scotsman that shall not be named. Regardless, It is always very informative. This goes on for a few hours. Then there is the revealing of what we are all looking forward to, the afternoon cultural activity.

We were to visit a football stadium, followed by a wine tasting event. This partly sounded brilliant. I like wine, but I don't understand the appeal to Football. Now I know this may make some or even most of you who share the same industry as I to put this book down or even use the pages for checking the sharpness of your grass cutting cylinders, but I just don't get Football. I watch it only when England play in international events, and that is mostly to have an opposing team to my wife, who does like Football and is Swedish. My sport has always been golf. I have played it to a very high level. My winter sport when I was young was Rugby. You can probably guess by now that I am a public schoolboy. I spent most of my younger years living in Africa and when the school I attended did not teach any older years I was sent to boarding school in the UK. So forgive my lack of understanding of Football. Those customers that work with us in Football just except that I will walk past a player I say "Hi mate" because I have no idea who they are. I think my ignorance amuses them.

Anyway, I digress again. You will get used to this.

After the conference, I zip up to my room to grab the few coins I had saved from a previous trip to Europe. I needed to get a packet of cigarettes from the vending machine, and it only took coins. When I get to my room, I discover that my room is remarkably clean, and so early in the day too. But the reason it is so neat was now apparent. I had paid for it with my Euros left on the desk. Such a schoolboy travel error. Anyway, my towels had been replaced with nice clean new ones.

Swearing slightly to myself I went downstairs and joined the others. I would sort my nicotine addiction later. It was time to get into a small bus and visit the stadium. I had been told that we were to see two enormous birds there. The finale was to be a club museum tour, to look at the trophies and other club memorabilia.

The tour is quite brief. We look at the pitch, which is nice and of high quality. We are not allowed to walk on the grass, which one would never do without permission anyway, and it looked in excellent condition.

We move to the changing room for the away team, which just smelt of men. Sitting down where the players change, we are offered to try the virtual reality headsets to show us the changing room of the hosts, which is almost the same and still smelt of men.

I wanted to see the big birds. So I got up and edged my way to the exit to the pitch. We walk out of the team tunnel and ok, I will admit here, the Eagle is a huge bird when you get close. It is magnificent and majestic. And the two that guard this stadium are just that. Sitting there on their perches, the birds do not look real. But they are, and when they spread their wings, you get a sneak peak of how scary they may look flying towards you on the attack at speed. I take lots of photos of them with the pitch in the background. I could have stayed there for some time just watching them. Sadly we had to leave the birds to go to the museum.

Well, what can I say? If you want a review of the museum, then do not ask me. I walked around the two-level museum and photographed a car, a razor, some bikinis, and coloured in a Christmas tree card in the Children's section. I went out for a smoke that I had been given from one of the other guys. I toured the whole museum in under ten minutes.

The wine tasting was next. You may have guessed by now that in my mind this was the more interesting of the two events set for the afternoon activity.

Arriving in the city centre the vibe is brilliant and bustling with life. I am not entirely sure I would like to drive here daily, as the streets are very narrow, cobbled, and full of parked fire engines and old police cars. Only the area around the wine bar had this but anyway. We arrive at the top of one of the seven hills that surround Lisbon. We walk down the hill to a brilliant little wine bar called *By The Wine* where wine bottles cover all the walls and the roof. The bar itself featured at the time of writing to be in the top 15 best bars in the city. I am now happy.

There was a section of the room set aside for us with wine bottles, dried meats and sumptuous cheeses. There was also a man to explain the wine and to go through how it was grown. The man walked around and occasionally handed out a thimble of wine to us to breathe in.

Ok, this is not entirely how it went.

Yes, we had the cheese and meat, and yes there was a man, but he told us the name of the wine that we were to taste and then gave us half a glass each and left—occasionally popping back to us to top up with another type of wine which, he informed us, was different from the previous one.

Having left the bar, we head back up the hill to the bus for our trip back to the hotel. The driver takes us on a very scenic drive along the city's riverfront with comments of things we passed, including a beer museum oddly. There were moans from the bus such as

"Why did you not book that? It would have been better than the dribbles of wine".

Back at the hotel, we have a short time before the group is to recoup and walk down to the reserved dinner restaurant, only a few hundred meters down the road.

We walk into the restaurant, all eighteen of us. I don't know why.

It was apparent that the place was rammed full with not a single table free. We were not going to fit in. We take a little piss out of our guide, and he insists that not only had the restaurant been booked in good time, but their office had prepaid. So they had to sort it out and we were not allowed to go into town to find somewhere else.

We are offered some potent drinks and sit outside under heated lamps like freshly prepared food. We were all quite shocked at what we could see through the window to the restaurant. To our astonishment, the waiters and waitresses were relocating customers halfway through their dinner to make a table big enough to accommodate all of us.

A little embarrassing for us all, we get ushered to our table. Our food arrives, which is a delicious selection of dishes. We drink all the wine and leave.

On returning to the hotel, we all ascend to the rooftop bar to say another hello to gin and tonic. I was a little disappointed that I had not seen any of the things I wanted to see in the city. But I felt that it was too late to go back into town for a wander promising myself that I would certainly come back to Lisbon as it looks like a beautiful city to explore more.

On arriving at the airport in Lisbon, the first thing you notice is that it is only half-open. I get this, it is a holiday destination, and thus unnecessary to use all of it all year round. The terminal we are in looked like the inside of a big aircraft hanger. The bit passed the passport control was smaller and looked like the inside of a shed.

Onboard our aircraft we were all sat close together again. This gave those who did not have to drive on the other side the opportunity to indulge in those cheese crackers I mentioned earlier. With wine.

Now I have had odd conversations on flights before, in fact, in many places. But our topic was nakedness and flying. Pluses include the speeding up of security, and the general reduction in flying due to embarrassing bodies. Would I fly as often as I do if I had to be naked for the duration? Probably not. You can discuss.

With a two-hour train trip back home, it is the start of the year's travel. Next week Yorkshire, and the City of Harrogate.

2. Harrogate UK January 2019

Every year I know where I am going to be in the third week of January. Maybe some of you readers do too—the Harrogate show for turf managers, BTME (British Turf Management Exhibition).

Harrogate is a town that sits in the middle of nowhere, surrounded by nothing exciting. A very wealthy city by all accounts. But it is where thousands of Greenkeepers and Groundsman gather together with trade manufactures of all kinds to hear about new technology and drink copious amounts of most of the drinks known to mankind. I feel sorry for the city dwellers at this time of the year.

It is always a busy few days, and everyone who is anyone in the turf industry in attendance. We, as a company, tend to host an evening for customers and have numerous meetings throughout the days.

I generally fly to Leeds/Bradford airport. The highest and one of the most scary airports to land at this time of year. I have, in the past, come in sideways, or landed after a few attempts. Welcoming you into the airport though are massive posters stating that the airport is the hub for "Connecting Yorkshire to the rest of the world". Poor world! As a Yorkshire born lad I can say this. Flying into Leeds Bradford International airport from Heathrow is, however, cheaper and more convenient than the train.

The hotel that we stay shall remain nameless. We have used it for years as a company base solely for its prime location to the show. It is directly opposite the main entrance, and since we use a boardroom there, it is perfect.

What is not perfect are the rooms, I have never had a good room there. It is basically a dog basket with en-suite. One year a man, very similar to the waiter and bellboy at a well known TV Torquay hotel, knocked on my room and told me in his broken English that I had no towels. I said that I had some, and they were fine, but he disagreed and walked into the room, passed me, and looked at them. Genuinely confused, he looked back and forth on his sheet of paper and then just left. It was pure comedy.

This year we found that the hotel had undergone a renovation. Well, it certainly needed it. I was looking forward to the upgrades. I discovered that my room was a newly painted dog basket with en-suite. But this year it did have a substantial quantity of white fluffy towels, and the plumbing had most definitely had a man look at it. I judge hotels solely on their towels. It is the one thing that makes such a difference. That is not wholly true; there are other things I look for in a hotel's star rating. But towels are the one thing that can redeem the hotels' other failures.

New this year also was the show set up and appearance in the conference centre. The rooms where the trade stands were to be the main difference. We had always had the same spot. It was easy to navigate to and in the section where many attendees of the exhibition walked by. Now I had to locate our new place. All I knew was that we were in the purple zone.

Thankfully I discover our stand reasonably quickly and got right down to business. Within minutes I had seen several customers from varying countries passing by our stand. Making several meeting arrangements to see them I caught up with the rest of the sales team. After a coffee and a good chin-wag I had to meet our MD to interview a few people for some sales rep positions in the UK. So back to the hotel I went.

Falling into the early evening, the meetings I had booked came to an end, and I slipped into the hotel bar. We had a well-deserved end of day beer and disappeared to our rooms to prepare for our company dinner at a restaurant around the corner, where we had booked seating for 60 with me having 18 customers from all over Europe attending. It was going to be a busy and stressful evening.

The dinner went well with great food, wine, and company. And it went on until we split at about 11 pm. As I had meetings booked for the whole following day I said my goodbyes and went to my basket for some sleep.

Up early for breakfast, I met up with some of my colleagues in the vast room that served both as a ballroom for Saga holidays and as a breakfast room for everyone else. I was pleased to see that they had removed the buffet and replaced it with table service. A new part of the renovations I guessed. They had some fruit and prunes you could help yourself, but since I don't have issues with my bowels, I left the prunes and ordered a fry up.

Eventually, my breakfast arrived, and I introduced it to the one-sided toast I had made using the world's most backward toaster machine. I had been told that the plate was hot by the waitress. I did not know that I would leave the skin on it when I moved it slightly further away from me—reducing the chances of setting my shirt on fire. Seriously, Did they add raw ingredients to it and then put the whole plate into a furnace? And it was not very edible anyway. It is hard to ruin an English breakfast, but they can do it. I grabbed some fruit and left.

The day of meetings was broken up with a one and a half hour lunch break for which, after looking a little around the rest of the trade show, I had with a colleague. It was a welcomed break as we had been talking all morning and the afternoon was to be relentless with my final meeting ending at 6:30 pm.

My last day was a travel day so my final evening could be a little more relaxed than the previous. But still, I did have an early morning taxi to the airport so one must be sensible. After all, I had been coughing like an idiot for the past five weeks, and this day had not made it any better. Could it have been the Corona virus back then? We will never know.

I had arranged to take some Norwegian customers that did not attend the previous evenings event out for an Indian meal. Always a pleasant and usually great fun gang and not one of them is Norwegian, they are typically Scottish or English but live and work in Norway. We amused ourselves over one of the guys latest trend of finding a female partner online. He was using a simple app that he swiped a specific direction to get conversation, and the other to ignore the match.

One such girl he was interested in started to chat while the food began to arrive on the table. Now I have been out of the dating world for many years, so I asked him how easy is it to meet up, and does he get much luck in finding a relationship that can last. He responded simply by saying that you have to be direct. If you want something for a weekend or a night or longer, you must say upfront.

By the end of the meal, he had received pictures of this girl. Some had clothes, and some did not! Both he and she were very direct.

Looking at the pictures Duncan, a customer of mine asked him.

"she is direct! And ready for you. What is her name?"

As I was sitting next to him, I leaned over and looked at his phone. On top of this profile was her name, "Edit".

I started to cough and laugh and could stop neither. He tried to explain to the rest of us that her name was Edith, but she had made a typing error on her profile. The laughter was immense around the table. We wished him well with their future, and I paid the bill. We went in search of a nightcap and then after a final drink we split up.

I met Beth, a colleague, in the lobby early the following morning. She was joining me to the airport. After checking out of the hotel the taxi driver to the airport arrived in a comfortable looking Mercedes. Unfortunately he had a habit of over exaggerating every aspect of his driving to the point of making Beth almost sick in the back. Thankfully we arrived before anything emerged.

On arrival at the airport, we briskly went through security and headed for the quiet lounge so we could grab some breakfast and a coffee. Both of us were extremely exhausted. We ignored each other and sat with our thoughts, longing for home.

I was looking forward to almost two weeks of working from home. This would be the break before a very hectic travel itinerary—an itinerary which would take me to seven counties over five weeks. This was to be the first test to see how much travel can work both for myself and the family.

3. Jersey February 2019

This trip was to be the first of many with the Agronomist. I have known him for a while now, and we got on well, so the travel would be quite easy. This is especially important as we were to be going to spend quite a bit of time together over the coming weeks. I even recall our MD phoning me to ask if my wife knew I was having an affair with him. We would be spending almost five weeks together in numerous countries with the weekends back in the UK.

Flying in from Scotland the Agronomist and I were to meet in Gatwick Airport for our short flight over to Jersey. I took the train that morning direct to the airport from Bosham where I live. One hour and no issues with parking or traffic the trip is a breeze. Although I am not so keen on Gatwick airport for business use, it is the only airport that British Airways uses to fly to Jersey.

On the train I sit opposite a girl, no older than eighteen, I guess. I kid you not she had about sixteen inches of makeup on. And then she decided this was not enough, so she borrowed some more from her friend and continued to cake it on for two stops. I know I sound old writing this, but there must be a limit on when you can't see your face and that enough is enough.

Through security at Gatwick, the Agronomist and I meet for breakfast at one of the many grill places in the departure lounge. We order a hearty breakfast, and I fill him in on the guys we were to meet. He had not been to Jersey before, so he got a little history lesson from me. Most of the information I forced into him came from a previous trip I had done with the seed company mentioned in the first chapter.

Jersey is not very big. You can cycle it in a day if you push it. There are many sports cars on the island of the rich. This is strange as the top speed you can go is 40MPH for about two mins on the only stretch of dual carriageway that exists just outside of St Helier. And speeding is heavily policed.

During the Second World War, Jersey was the only part of the British Isles that was taken over by the Germans, and there were many propaganda pictures made up by the Germans to give a little hint of what the rest of the UK would be like under their rule. The museum is worth visit just for these. I informed the Agronomist of the Nigel Mansell Museum, where you can have a headset guide, made by Nigel himself, to take you around the room filled with everything "the Nigel" was given, won, or bought. And he goes in to great detail about each item.

Finished with our breakfast, and since his eyes were beginning to wonder, we walk around the fragrance section in the duty-free shop trying to locate a new one for me. I discovered that my last smell was used also by a colleague. And because I have since then run out, I had refused to buy it again. We checked out a few to replace it and after criticising many with such comments as "well that smells of a man in an open-top sports car with his shirt half undone exposing his hairy chest" we left.

No wiser, we went for the brief fortnight walk to our plane. Travelling with people is hard if they are not sure or travel infrequently. One needs space and time alone on these moments. Well, I do, anyway. Thankfully we can't be arsed to sit next to each other on planes unless we fancy having a beverage or two. We like to put on the noise-cancelling headphones and emerge ourselves in audiobooks or music and meet when we get off the plane.

Having arrived, we are picked up by Kevin, a customer of mine, and taken to the golf course he manages five minutes from the runway where we were to have our presentation.

With everything having gone well and having spent some good quality time with customers there, we take the opportunity to introduce Kevin as the new employee and representative for our company in Jersey. Both myself and the Agronomist would continue to give support. But it would fall mostly on Kevin's shoulders from now on for local sales and support.

We made plans to meet a few of the guys in the evening and left with our new colleague and onwards to our hotel.

I have stayed several times in Jersey at a few different hotels but The Radisson Waterfront is by far the best one I have experienced. And with it being off-season the prices were excellent. Being a gold member of their reward program, I received an upgrade, and what an upgrade it was.

My room, sorry apartment, was only on the first floor but it overlooked the rainy and windy waterfront. I only found out about the view from bay windows when I walked through the hall, then the office and living room, and then on to the bedroom. It is so wonderful to have a room like this when staying in a hotel. Annoyingly it was to be for one night only as we were to leave early in the morning. So having used both of my bathrooms, I went down to the lobby bar to gloat about my room and have a drink with the Agronomist.

We walk over the harbour towards the city centre and directly into my favourite bar in St Helier. The Lamplighter, an excellent traditional pub that is most definitely frequented by visitors and locals alike. It boasts about a hundred different whiskies on its board and numerous beers on tap. We had a few beers and grabbed a bag of Biltong, my favourite bar snack ever. Originally from South Africa, this dried beef is a perfect accompaniment with beer. Within the bag, there is a small little moisture-retaining or controlling pouch. Surprising enough it has "do not eat" written all over it in numerous languages. We discussed the things needed to stop a lawsuit from the stupid that never ceases to amaze me. The meat is succulent and spicy.

The following morning the weather had not reduced its battering on the island. And by all accounts it was to worsen. Saying that, there were no mentioned delays, so we headed for the airport. Just after check-in, I checked my App for the latest on the flight situation. Sure enough, the flight was delayed due to the incoming flight from London being delayed leaving Gatwick, also due to bad weather.

We walked around the airport for something to do. Having completed this in ten minutes, we found some lunch and settled down to work separately on our laptops. With everything caught up and the weather still being relentless, we decided to have a drink. It was just after lunchtime and I was taking the train home on the other side, and him staying in London for the weekend, so we chilled out with a beer. We discussed why there was a "passenger disruption desk" at the airport. It was clear to us that if there were passengers disrupting things, they would remove them, wouldn't they? And I cant imagine disruptive passengers quietly queuing in a line to do so.

Anyway, we finally saw our plane coming into the terminal and praised its quick turnaround. We boarded and then looked forward to our weekend back in the UK. Next week we meet in Oslo, Norway.

4. Norway February 2019

It was in the local pub that, while chatting to a mate called Paul, I discover that he was flying on the following day from Gatwick to Edinburgh. I was off to Norway by Norwegian Air, which incidentally at the time of writing has one of the best onboard internet services. The luck was that I no longer had to take the early morning commuter train, which is so busy and dirty and full of business people ignoring each other. We could have an excellent breakfast and chill out before the flight. Paul's flight was a little earlier than mine, but that was fine. I also was to meet the Agronomist as he was flying in from Glasgow and meeting me at the airport.

The Agronomist and I were supposed to be on the same flight. It turned out I was on the 9:20, and he was on the 11:20. This was slightly annoying as we both wanted to drive the hire car in Oslo. Furthermore, I was under time pressure as I had two customer visits followed by a drive on to Sweden to spend the night with my colleague Peter in his summer house, while the Agronomist spent the evening with his brother and his wife in Oslo.

The reason for my trip to Sweden was that I needed to have a quick meeting with my Swedish bank for our upcoming family move back to Sweden. Irritatingly something I could not do on the phone or the internet, I had to physically show my face at a branch in Sweden.

Having spent a pleasant night in Sweden with Peter, who I had not seen for a while, I was left to lock the cottage up and head back to Norway via the bank to meet the Agronomist. We then were to carry on with two other visits that day, before heading to our hotel in the city.

The Scandic Vulcan in Oslo is a great place to stay. Quite central but not in the idiotic hard to park areas of the city, right next to the Oslo food market. I like this area as you have small bars and restaurants close to one of my favourite places to eat, *Bar Social.* The car parking is also just opposite the hotel and cheaper than others but still expensive by European standards.

With a reasonably quick shower and change, we met up in the lobby and walked over to the *Bar Social* for dinner. After a fantastic feed, we felt that a quick drink in the bar opposite would be a good idea. The entrance to this bar is not apparent. You walk down some slippery stairs following the coloured lights and then pull back the heavy metal door. There are no windows that we could see, we wanted to know what the place would be like before entering. We don't want to walk into an empty bar. The location of the bar is situated on the side of the riverbank so there is no option to check before. We walked in holding our breath.

On entering we see that there is about a fifty-meter long bar with options of tapped beers from around Norway and a few from other countries too. There are also boards and boards with long lists of cocktails to choose. The music was on, and we liked it. The bar was neither full nor empty so we ordered drinks. The barman asked to pay upfront, which I don't like doing. The barman slid the card machine in front of me and hovered for an awkward moment before starting to pull our beer. We conversed together and ignored him. In my opinion, this is not the sort of thing you do. I waited until the drinks were delivered before I put the card close for the machine to read the contactless chip. As I did the device "timed out". This was to the barman's displeasure, and he moved from a friendly, polite, albeit direct barman to now a direct and irritated barman. He set the machine up again to receive my payment.

While we ignored him and discussed the rest of the bar, the music was starting to gain our attention. The tunes were good. They were a collection of classic hits mixed with modern chart-toppers. But all of the songs had one thing in common. They were all abruptly ended by the DJ just before they finished. It was tune after tune the same. Now, this was beginning to irritate the Agronomist very much.

Waking back from the toilet, I handed the evening's music quiz question paper to the Agronomist, and he looked at it and then me with an "Ahh".

Day three of the week-long visit took us to three golf courses, meeting our customers and the Agronomist meeting them for the first time in a very long time. Since he took over the agronomical services side to our company, he had not been back to Norway other than to visit family members. We wanted to go through the new services we were offering and have a course walk at each. We were to meet up with the same guys for dinner in the Åker Brugge part of Oslo. Famed for its slightly more exclusive bars and restaurants it does have one bar that stands out from the crowd. The *Beer Palace* is a place you must have a beverage, even if only the one. This naturally depends on the depth of your pockets. A night out here can cost quite a packet.

There are many top-class restaurants around, but we had decided upon an American diner-style place called *Burger House* for food, which was not supposed to be that expensive in comparison. And in contrast to others, it was not. The burger menu suggested an average of €30 per dish, with the sides coming extra on top. The place looked clean, busy, and enjoyable.

Not to go mad we all ordered a burger, fries and coleslaw. This went with one beer each.

The Burgers duly arrived, and we were all very impressed. I was looking forward to devouring my "New Yorker" right up to the moment I filled my plate with A1 Sauce. I had forgotten that it has the same consistency as water. Thus with a huge glug, the dish was covered. With laughter over and my food having one single flavour, we agreed that it was a great burger. The thimble of coleslaw was a disappointment, but what the hell, it was all about the burger.

We had agreed to have one last beer back at the *Beer Palace*. I ordered the bill and even though our burgers were very reasonably priced the coleslaw was the equivalent of €4. It was the size of the small marmalade jar. The ones you get in shit country hotels where they do this to make you feel that no expense has been spared to give you individuality, but in actuality, every expense has been spared with no care for the environment.

Feeling ripped off, I said nothing about it to the waiter and agreed everything was fantastic and left.

The fourth day in Norway and it was to be another busy one. We had four courses to visit with a good deal of driving between them on winter roads. While on the way to the first course we had a call that one of the course managers was home ill with his child so would have to cancel for the day. This meant we had more time to spend with the first two meetings and a less stressful drive between them with the tight schedule we had.

During the first visit, we had a call from one of our Swedish colleagues, and he wanted to have a photo of the Agronomist for the website and to use in promotional material for his upcoming presentations in Sweden. So with a good background of a white wall in the workshop, I took a few pictures and sent them on.

Moving on, we completed our second visit and planned our drive up to Hønefoss, a beautiful part of Norway an hour out of the city of Oslo. With its gushing river flowing through the city centre we drove the fantastically picturesque road up out of the town and passes Tyrifjord. We were not to go to the golf club situated on the island but we were to meet Ian, the course manager. I often stay with him while on my visits, but this time it was Valentine's Day and we refused his kind offer to do so as we felt it was an encroachment on his valentines with his wife.

We arrived at the Scandic Hotel in Hønefoss and duly checked in and received our rooms. I noted that the electricity was a good two meters away from the bed, which is always annoying. In this day and age, we are used to our phones being next to the bed, I know for me it is the last thing I stoke at night and the first in the morning too. Well, almost.

We meet up in the bar and grab a drink before deciding where to go for dinner. Being Valentines, we thought that an Indian meal would be great, and not so full of romantic couples having time together. The closest was a two minute walk from the hotel entrance. It looked quite empty as we had hoped. We order the fish curry and a spicy sizzling chicken dish with a few naan breads. But only after we had waited, and had been ignored, for about ten minutes. We order a couple of beers too. These beers took soo long that we immediately ordered another two on arrival. The food is eaten up quickly and is delicious.

Back at the hotel, we have a few games of pool then hit the sack. We had decided that since the last visit on Friday was cancelled due to the illness of the course manager, the Agronomist had changed his flight to an earlier one so he could spend a little more time with his children. He was having a long weekend in Norway to celebrate one of his daughters birthdays. They live in the far North of Norway with his ex-partner. We were to meet in Prague in two weeks so we kind of had enough of each other and wanted to be home with our families.

We hit the icy roads towards the airport and arrive in good time for his flight to the North. We handed the car back and parted company. There was no point for me to go through security and spend the day in the lounge, so I found a cosy cafe and got to work. It was an excellent chance to get everything up to date in my inbox and catch up with the boss on the phone.

Mid-morning I receive an email from the hire company with pictures of a less than 2 cm scratch on the wheel arch of the car. This was to cost NOK 2500 (approx £250 at time of writing) which was ludicrous. Regardless, I had a credit card that covered all insurance issues with car hire companies. I had no idea how to use it as this was the first time it had ever happened. I was, and still am, adamant that it was not me. It did give me the idea always to video the car before I leave the hire car station in the future though. A habit that I continue to this day.

With two hours until my flight back to London, I went through security and headed for the lounge where I discovered that my flight was going to be delayed. Great! After spending most of the day at the airport, I was now to spend even longer. But at least I had free wine and food to keep me going.

With another week away, I looked forward to getting home. It is to be Rome and Milan next week, so I looked forward to that. The negative thing with this upcoming trip was that it was smack across the half term week and not so popular with the family. Still, I would make it up with a long stint working from home later in the year.

5. Italy February 2019

First stop Rome. The week was to be split between a conference of The European Greenkeepers Association in Rome followed by a trade show in Milan with a distributor of ours. I had been looking forward to this trip as I had never visited the ancient city of Rome before. Having pre-booked my Vatican Museum and Basilica tour to skip the waiting line of people, I had planned a little tour of Rome in the evening prior to the event.

Having arrived at the airport, I take a somewhat reliable fast train to the city. I love walking around cities as you get a good feeling of local life, the smell, the sounds, and the vibe. The hotel was a pleasant 30 min walk through the streets of old Rome.

The hotel I had booked, which would be brilliant if I could remember the name of, was right on the doorstep of the parliament building, something that I did not realise until I arrived at it. It is impossible to walk down a street and not see something interesting in this town. It is an open-air museum.

I grab a shower and hit the streets. Rome City is impressive. If you have not been, then you need to. I proceeded to start what would be my 9 km walk throughout the evening with a first visit to the Trevi Fountain. It was rammed with tourists all throwing their coins in for good luck. Surprising nobody gets hurt actually. I threw mine too. Not completely understanding what it does, I thought my wish. I do know that they scoop up nearly 2500Euros a day, so it certainly gives a good income to the city.

I thought about buying some sort of token to remind me of my trip. I often do, and the items vary in what they are and how relevant to the place I am visiting varies. Options for Rome could include a Christian cross, a piece of rock, or some Holy water perhaps. I even considered buying a wooded giraffe from one of the many African guys that have portable stalls around the city. But since I have lived in East Africa, I have one already, so I moved on not buying anything.

I found a restaurant close to the fountain. It is always slightly awkward walking into a restaurant and asking for a table for one.

Dinner was possibly the best Lasagne I have ever had, with the service being equally excellent. I continue to walk around visiting The Pantheon, The Spanish Steps, The Colosseum, and numerous other 2000-year-old buildings. Looking for some bar to grab a nightcap. I end up somehow right outside a building, in a side street, with a load of paparazzi gathered outside. I ask them what the situation is and they inform me that the far-right Nationalist Party were having some sort of meeting. I left them to it and walked on and without knowing exactly where I was, arriving at my hotel only 50 m up the road.

Not finding a bar on the way I thought I would grab a wine in the hotel bar before bed. The only other people in the bar were a British couple arguing and comparing what the problems with Brexit were. One voted differently to the other. Half listening, I watch the news on the television while sipping my wine. I was very amused by the English couple's comments and went out for a cigarette worrying about it, and them. It just shows how much people don't know and yet still are passionate about what they believe is right.

Outside I admired the locale, and while I was enjoying the smoke, I am approached by a young girl who wanted to borrow my lighter to light her massive cigar. I mean this was a girl, about 24 years old, Russian, with one of the biggest cigars I have seen.

We chatted for a bit; I smoked about five cigarettes, and when she finished the cigar, we went inside. I say chatted, but we talked through the new translating app on my phone. So I got my £4.99 worth anyway. It almost worked perfectly. She had apparently been given a trip by her parents for her birthday and had always wanted to visit Rome. She enlightened me into how life was for her in Moscow and how she was trying to set up a business in fashion. I am not sure she understood what I did for a living nor I think she cared. It got quite late and since I had a date with The Pope early in the morning, I went to bed with a feeling quite light headed.

The Vatican is also a must-see being the smallest country in the world. Good to tick that off my list of countries visited. My only advice is to book online. There are many touts around offering discount tickets, VIP tours, and more Africans selling giraffes. Booking the audio guide means you skip the two-week queue and this is essential.

After two hours roaming around the wonderful museums, it is time to get back to work. My next mission was to get to the conference which was closer to Rome airport than the city. Now I had heard that the taxis were expensive, so I thought I would walk back to the central train station and grab an airport train-which turns out to be a three-week walk from the main terminal- and then take the ten-minute taxi ride to the hotel that the conference was situated. The train passed through some of the outskirts of the city and one can see the stark change from old to modern architecture.

It turned out that I was to spend 15Euro more doing this and waste two hours of my life. So much for trying to save the company money.

The Sheraton at the airport, where the conference was, has a golf course. I have to say that I did not see it at all during the entire stay. But it was time to get right into the work-mode of networking again.

First stop is the hotel bar, naturally. I met and conversed with a few people I know from various parts of Europe and the industry. It was nice to catch up.

Having showered, changed and struggled to put a bow tie on, I was back to the hotel bar and more networking, this time I joined a number of Scandinavians and we had various languages around us. I do speak Swedish and thus can converse pretty ok in Norwegian and understand Danish with concentration. We had other parts of Scandinavia join our table, namely Finnish and Icelandic so the language switched to English as it was too complicated and by this time far too much wine had been consumed anyway.

Dinner was to be in the clubhouse of the golf course I did not see and was a short bus ride away. The ride made even shorter and more memorable by the fact that the driver did not like to use the brake very much. It was full-speed in all directions. We came to an abrupt halt. He must have finally found the brake pedal. We fell out the back, and slightly dizzy with motion sickness I went in search of more wine, more networking and some food, which was very good indeed. After a formal dinner with speeches and welcome introductions it was time to leave for the hotel again.

The way back was equally entertaining as we waited for the arrival of the bus. It was not there to greet us as promised. We started to walk back to the hotel after some time freezing waiting. With new friends, we spoke and exchanged business cards and plans for visits and meetings. We talked about the following days of the conference and then I went to bed quite exhausted.

At 8 am we are ushered onto another bus to go to the 2022 Rome Ryder Cup course which was, at the time of writing, under construction. In fact, the whole place was, for the most part under either construction or in need of renovation. Still, there is time, and I look forward to seeing it on the television.

After the day of group activities where there were discussions of future Greenkeeping practices and new research in all aspects of turf management, we went into Rome City for a group dinner. The organiser planned on taking us all to a restaurant he had booked. We arrive and discover we are very early. While we waited for our reservation we are told we could find a bar for a pre-dinner drink in the proximity. We split up and went in search of a bar. Most of the bars are quite small and cosy and it was probably good we all split into smaller groups.

I had to stop to grab some cigarettes on the way so "my" group that I shall introduce shortly lost the rest of the delegates. But since we were equipped with modern smartphones, we were not bothered in the slightest. We knew where the restaurant was and the time our reservation was booked for so it was time to explore.

We found a bar that was advertising "Porno Shots". And we thought that it would be a great idea to have one. How to describe them? Well, they are like swallowing a punk rock band that all have knives instead of instruments. I don't recommend them. A few beers later, we went in search of the restaurant.

I should introduce our little band of merry European and afar Sales Managers/Representatives or whatever you like to call us. There are four of us, Caroline, Lee, Jos, and myself.

After dinner, or should I say banquet, I mean I have never eaten so many full plated courses in my life, we picked up a few extra guys in our group, Joel, A Portuguese guy and board member of the association we are all gathered for, Jim, a very well known British greenkeeping authoritarian and one more whom I forget his name, sorry. We decided that the night was far too young for us and went search for drinks and a bit of Roman nightlife.

After a few more "Porno Shots," beers, and Rose wine; there was nothing left open in Rome, so it was time to go.

We had hoped that the guys had picked up our bags from the bus and left them at the hotel reception. They had not. Now Caroline had realised that her wallet had gone too. Upset, and slightly under the influence, I suggest that she cancel her cards, or at least put a temp block on them until the morning. She was to stay the weekend to take in the sights of Rome. This is not ideal without a wallet. I had a spare bank card that she could use so she could transfer online cash to that. I had no money in it anyway, so did not need it. She could then post the card to me the following week. All was sorted and nothing to worry about. Happier we both went to get some sleep. The bags we would deal with the next morning.

The morning came around with the feeling of sandpaper in my mouth. The punk rock band had now moved to my head and replaced the knives with stones. I went in search of water and some breakfast. I located the bags which had been put in our conference room and immediately was relieved. My life was in my satchel. Passports, WiFi, Notebook, Ipad and Phones.

Now I call it a satchel. Everyone who knows me calls it a "man bag". I do get a lot of stick about it. And probably will do more now. But regardless I had it, and all was well.

Caroline was relieved too with my discovery as I had also found out that Joel had her wallet! But he did not have her number to let her know. He had left earlier than us the previous night and taken it with him. We sill have no idea how he had her wallet.

To catch my flight to Milan, I left after lunch. I looked forward to an evening wandering around again, grabbing some early dinner and then having a non-alcohol night to be fresh enough for the show and meeting our distributor there.

Well, it turned out to be fashion week also in Milan, so there were hundreds of oddly dressed people at the airport on my arrival. I mean a mid 50 years old man in tight white jeans which were 3 inches short showing his bare foot slipped inside of some gleaming shoes with green tassels on them is just not fashion to me. It is stupid and opens the door to piss-take at the highest level. If I turned up looking like that at certain golf clubs in Norway, I would make the Green-keepers literally burst with laughter.

Outside the terminal building, everyone wanted a taxi. This just added to the congestion of every car in Milan wishing to use the same road at the same time. What could be a 20 min drive into town from the "city" airport took almost 2 hours, and 30 Euros. Now I was getting frustrated, and my plans were going out of the window very fast.

Just to top it off the hotel was shit. It was an office block blended with apartments and trade show booths. This was seriously worse than a Travel Lodge in the UK. And the price for this misery?, are you sitting down? 158Euros! During fashion week it seems like the price of everything triples in Milan.

I did not even bother with a shower and went in search of a local restaurant for dinner. Outside my hotel is the Basilica with Leonardo's "The Last Supper". Not being able to see it for real, I walked on into town.

I found a nice little street restaurant which had a table outside. The waiter was attentive but quite sleazy towards a couple of girls opposite me, handing over his number and Facebook details. Not sure how appropriate that is really. Still, they did not seem to mind.

My wine and food arrived, and it was delicious. Both consumed within minutes. I wished to have an early night and looked forward to some sleep.

This was only to be lightly interrupted every 30 mins with toilet noises. The morning came and I was in a bad mood. I picked up the bill for the hotel, with a forklift truck, and then spent another fortune on a taxi to the show ground.

It also seems that taxi drivers do not like cards. I think Italians don't like plastic payments, which is odd because American Express is advertising everywhere. I had to stop to take cash out the wall on the way. Something I should never do on the company card, but since I had left the PIN to my new Swedish debit card at home I had no choice, and Caroline had my other debit card with no money on it.

The Show Ground in Milan is enormous, I mean big. Massive in fact. Think big and then add some. It was full of football pitch size rooms filled individually with trade shows from shoes, glasses, leather ("the natural choice"), and finally Plants and Garden stuff.

I was to be in the My Plant and Garden show and had to locate our company distributor in one of the three big rooms that the show consisted. The set up was excellent. And as soon as I had stopped walking around for 15 mins in the wrong place, I found them and was offered a coffee. The show was excellent, and although many Italians don't speak English as fluently as Scandinavians, I conversed with several people and made some new connections.

At noon, when in other shows I have attended there is a low point of footfall through, the drinks and lunch bitings come out on the stand. There is Prosecco, beer, Salami, olives, bread, and Parmesan cheese with a finger lime jam. What a great idea.

Now I will go on about this lime jam a bit. It is like a drop of heaven has been placed upon the Parmesan. You need to find it. It is rare and quite expensive. You can put it on fish, lobster, cheese, and even in Prosecco. You need it in your life.

I said my goodbyes and left the show just after it closed to head for the airport. Now I had spent a lot taking taxis this week and felt quite bad about it. I had tried many ways to save the company cash. Now I was going to Uber it. I would take the risk. I checked, and it was 118Euros quote for a 23min drive!

This was ridiculous. I could not go to town by train, spend an hour all to save 40 Euros as I did not have time. I stood there looking at the standard Taxis all wanting to charge 145Euros for the same and then came a man, whom can only be described as looking like one of the Blues Brothers. He offered me a choice. 80 Euros cash or 88 Euros by card. They say it is like this only on Milan fashion week. And I agree, rip the fuckers off who are daft enough to wear clothes that don't work.

In the taxi, I discover that the guy had issues other than his clothes sense. He just clapped for no reason when some shit song came on the radio. Nodding and tapping along with the tunes he swerved lanes like there was no end and no other traffic. Then he started writing text messages and emails and WhatsApp messages. I observed his eyes and could see we would travel 50 to 60 m before he would lookup. We only got beeped at twice in the 19 mins I was in the car with him. Why did I not say anything to him? I just don't know.

At the airport, I was relieved to get out. Friday night travel is not fun. I had a 8 pm flight to London which would mean that would be home by 11:30 pm. What a week. But all back again next week with a 3:30 am start on Monday morning for a flight to Vienna...Jealous?

6. Austria and Czech Rep February 2019

After a weekend most alone at home it was an early start to the week again. At 4 am the taxi picks me up and I sleep most of the way to Heathrow. I think that these weeks are catching up on me.

Arriving at Vienna airport I continued with my trying to save the company money by taking the train to the wrong place in the city having to take the underground metro to the station where my hire car actually was.

Do you know I have absolutely no idea what car it was. I can say that it was a Toyota and that's it.I only know this because of the logo on the steering wheel. I have started a new game and that unless I can guess the car from the instant I see it or from the interior then I will write about it. But If I don't then you, the reader, shall not know either. It was rubbish anyway so don't lose sleep over it.

Anyway, I videoed the car and checked it over for damages. One can say that there was Apple Car play installed and that it was dull to drive. The hotel I had chosen for this short trip to Vienna was called Daniel. It is easy to spot as it has a boat that looks like it is melting off of the roof and dripping down the side. It also boasts a Sunbeam caravan style thing that you can also book to sleep in as an option. Daniel is known for its appearance in the UK Channel 4 show with Richard Ayoade called Travel Man.

The room had a shower with a glass window so that your partner or colleague can watch you clean yourself whilst they sit on the bed. It also came with no desk. I do miss that. There are a few things I wish for in a hotel room. Large fluffy towels (preferably white), a desk with chair, and electricity next to the bed. These are my basic requirements. Richard Ayoade was given a much larger room with a desk whilst his guest, Chris O'Dowd, had the Sunbeam.

I went down for dinner and enjoyed a simple burger and a beer. I also enjoyed being in a WhatsApp conversation with a bunch or Norwegian customers of mine. At one point one of them sent a picture through that cannot be put in ink here that made me spit out my drink. Embarrassingly I cleaned the table with my napkin and continued to cough and giggle.

Back in my room I called American Express and sorted out the final bits for the insurance for the Hire Car incident in Norway. Such great service does Amex give it is worth mentioning them.

With an early morning drive round to see two customers, it was a full day updating them on new developments in our product range and also finalising their orders for the year. I had to get back to the city for the train I had booked to take me to Prague that evening. The train would take me on a relaxed ride to meet with the Agronomist who was flying in from Scotland.

Arriving at the drop off point for the hire car in one of many central stations in Vienna I videoed the car before leaving it and dropping the keys in a bin. I had pre-booked the ticket months ago and managed to get first class for €35. This was to include some sort of snack and drinks. Well, I thought this was extremely good value. It also included access to the lounge in the station. I had half an hour to spare before the train's departure so I went in it to see what it was like. No beer but there was a coffee machine and some fruit so I helped myself and sat down and read my book. Onboard I opened up the Ipad to catch up on final emails and sat down for a relaxing trip to Prague.

Prague's central station is quite a beautiful building. Built-in 1871 it has gone by a few names. Originally called the Franz Joseph after Franz Joseph 1 of Austria. During a renovation, it was renamed after a former President of the USA Woodrow Wilson. I don't know why. The station is a major international hub and very easy to navigate.

Arriving into the station I plan my walk through the streets towards the centre. From there I knew where my hotel was. Just over the other side of the Charles Bridge to the right. So with my bag bumping down the cobbled streets, I made my way.

I love the nightlife of Prague. It is relaxed, yet busy. Walking through the streets you feel safe and secure amongst such a mixture of people. You have your couples having a romantic walk and tourists wandering lost in the little side streets. Unfortunately you also have your groups of Hens and Stags. But they are easy to spot so also easy to avoid. The centre part of the city and the Square with the famous Astronomical clock situated on the side of the town hall also marks a good meeting point.

Just before I was to arrive into this square I decided to grab a break from the noise of my roller bag on the cobbled stones. The microbrewery is quite a new concept in the Czech Republic. You have your big brands naturally, but these smaller breweries are a must to try. The one, simply called *Beer Prague* is brilliant. You can get beer in a number of ways, and also if you are hungry you can grab a pork knuckle, a local delicacy that will both fill you up and help you immediately go to sleep afterwards.

After leaving the *Beer Prague* I follow a large group of tourists into the Staré Mesto, the old town square. They were being guided by a man with an umbrella. Walking past the clock tower on the town hall, I made my way through a few streets until the beginning of the Charles Bridge. I never get bored of crossing the river on this bridge. It truly is a sight. The towers either side and the eeriness of the mist over are just out of a movie. The only spoiler is the tourists and street stalls popping up over it. The many statues across have brass shiny bits on them to stroke. They give you luck if you do. Or maybe it is just disease, can't quite remember.

I checked into the Charles Hotel and listened to the most enthusiastic night manager ever. After describing many facilities he finally gave me my room key. Now, this hotel I have stayed before. It is in a perfect location for city visiting but it is very quirky. I mean the rooms have odd-shapes and there is always something that is just a little out of the ordinary. But I like it.

One such quirk is that my toilet was just a little too high for comfort. My legs did not quite reach the floor properly. Maybe the idea is to reduce the time spent on it. And I am not what I call short. If you are less than 180cm then you will have the feeling of a toddler being house trained.

I decide to go down to the underground bar and restaurant within the hotel to get some dinner before the Agronomist arrived. I was surprised to note that the ownership had changed hands. It was now a Chinese restaurant. I order a simple meal of noodles and some chicken in a sauce together with a nice cold Chang beer. Thinking this was going to be the only time ever I would eat here I may as well go all in and not have anything local at all.

Once the bill arrived I was shocked to discover that they did not take payment cards of any kind. It is quite unusual. Prague is a modern city and cards are widely accepted. I suggested that they just add it to my room. This was not possible either. I asked if they were serving breakfast on behalf of the hotel. "Yes" was the response I got. So then I said that I would pass by with cash as I had no Czech cash on me. This was fine as they took the number of my room. My plan was to pass by with cash and avoid their breakfast at all costs as the meal I had just eaten was not what I call up to scratch. The cold Chang beer was perfect though.

I went back up to my room and caught up with some more emails and waited for the Agronomist to arrive. He called a short while after to say that he was in a taxi and would be arriving at the hotel soon. I went outside for a smoke to wait for him.

Whilst having my cigarette I got talking to a friendly drunk guy who was very pleased to join me in smoking my cigarettes. He slurred through his points on the world and Czech politics until the Agronomist jumped out of his cab. Not being rude I introduced him to the drunk and then we left him outside with another one of my cigarettes to keep him company, and we went to check-in.

The Agronomist had not been to Prague before, and I was keen to be the tour guide of one of my favourite cities in the world. We took a walk over the Charles bridge and I suggested we pop in a music bar on the other side for a catch-up beer. I did not tell him that the bar had ladies in it hanging on poles.

After a good night sleep in our quirky rooms, we met up in the breakfast room/Chinese restaurant. I had not informed the Agronomist of the change of ownership since I was last there and he, not being the most alive of a morning, looked confused. He went in search of an egg and some bacon. He came back disappointed. I suggested noodles but he was not in the mood for my jokes and gave me a killer look. He had coffee in silence.

Our Czech distributor was to pick us up and take us to a new construction of a golf course where there was Jordan, an old colleague and friend of the Agronomist. He was the head man in fact and had used our companies products in his past roles and wanted to continue with that albeit through our distributor. It was also a good chance for the Agronomist to get back in contact with his old friend.

We had a good drive and walk about the golf course site, some sections were ready and others still piles of mud and trees. It is nice to see this in action. The changes over a fairly short period of time are amazing. We discussed how we were to supply him and what over a good lunch in a local brewery.

We got a lift back to the city with our distributor and decided to go for a walkabout. I suggested that we walk up to the spectacular St Vitus Cathedral that overlooks the city. It is the resting place of many Holy Roman Emperors and Bohemian kings and is part of the Prague Castle complex. It is a wonderful sight and full of gargoyles protecting it.

We walked up through the complex and down again the many steps towards the city. We stopped off in a local bar that was defiantly off the tourist route. We were given no option of drinks. We were ushered to a table and then given two beers and two shots of Becherovka to be washed down with the beer. It was very nice. The bill was even nicer as it cost less than €5 for it all.

We head back to the hotel to grab a shower and change before meeting up with Jordan, the course manager we had met during the day and also two others. One German guy, Tom, who had recently taken over another new construction and also Ben, a Brit who was course manager at the European Tour course just to the north of the city.

Whilst getting into my shower I discovered another quirky feature of my hotel room. So the toilet was designed for long-legged people I had discovered but the shower was just over waist height. How was this to work? You either make it for tall people or short people guys! And even the average height people are going to be irritated with not being able to get on the toilet or have a shower standing. Still, the hotel had a good location and I still like it.

We suggested to Tom, Jordan and Ben that we meet by the clock tower, as usual. On arriving it was time for the clock to strike and play its tune so there were hundreds of tourists gathered around with their mobile phones all pointed at the clock face waiting to record a little skeleton banging a chime.

Still, we found the guys and headed for the *Beer Prague* brewery that I had stopped off on my walk from the station the previous day.

The beer was good and so reasonably priced for being in the centre of Prague.

We had ordered a beer tasting wooden log with six types of beer on them and the pork knuckle. We discussed all the things four blokes do when they get together with meat and beer.

After dinner, we agreed to grab a last drink at the *Anonymous Bar*. This is a bar that is not actually marked. You need to find it. Or rather know where it is from someone else. Once you do find it you are directed to a table and then given a menu for which there are secret drinks hidden amongst the other offerings but you need to have a UV light to see them. I quite like the V blood in the way it arrives like an intravenous drip. You open the tap and the drink mixture empties itself slowly through the pipe into your glass filled with ice. A cool gimmick and you also get to take an Anonymous face mask home with you too. Mine now lives on my shelf of shit in my home office.

The next morning whilst trying to get the guy at reception to organise us a taxi we decide that we do not fancy a Chinese for breakfast so we went for the other non-standard local breakfast, a *McDonalds*. Horrible I know, but it was what we needed. We had a hangover to deal with.

The Taxi booking seamed like a hard thing to do. We wanted to visit Ben at his golf course before our flights home and it proved either too far and too complicated even though it is only 10 minutes from the main airport. Finally, we did convince the guy and he had to make a further last call to get a price he was to charge us.

Borat the taxi driver finally arrived. Not joking that was his name. He took us to the club and we had a great drive about even though it was very cold on the back of the buggy.

Ben then offered to drop us at the airport after a quick lunch of Czech cheese that is deep-fried. Not the most healthy of meals but oh so delicious.

We are dropped off at the airport and for the first time, I find my-self queuing in the line with the Agronomist to check-in without checking in myself. I was on a different airline and flying into London. He had a direct flight back to Scotland in an orange plane.

All in all a good visit to both Vienna and Prague with much work done. I looked forward to a few days of working from home with only a brief trip to Ireland the following week. A nice break to the even more hectic travel that is to come.

7. Dublin Ireland March 2019

The trip to Ireland is one I only do twice a year. It is to meet up with two sales guys that work for us covering N. Ireland and some parts of the Republic of Ireland. I was picked up by one of them at Belfast City airport, still posting the name George Best Airport after the famed footballer. We drove for a bit, catching up on the way with the local golf market and sales figures. We were to meet the other sales guy in a roadside service station half way from the airport to his place of work.

I suggested that food was in order as I had been awake since 3:15 am to get my flight with no margin at London at all for a pick-up and run breakfast.

With our sandwiches in front of us, we got right down to the figures and budgets. We discussed opportunities and pitfalls of the work and the industry. We were only interrupted by the occasional laugh by one of the workers in the cafe. It sounded like a fox making love. This was made slightly worse due to the fact the room was very echoey.

Following the meeting, I get a lift to the central train station in Belfast so I could make the trip to Dublin. I had wanted to do this for some time now. Also, with the Brexit issue still going on (it was two weeks to go at the time of my visit), I wished to experience the border crossing before whatever might be hindering it in the future.

Note: Brexit was not to happen on March 31st 2020, as we now know.

Belfast station is quite small for a central station but very easy to negotiate and filled with accommodating staff. I found that the trains in NI are so much nicer than the mainland UK ones and much cleaner and more comfortable too.

I enjoyed the countryside view while responding to some emails and putting orders into the office. What I was really looking for was the border. I kept looking on the map app on my phone. I don't know why, I just needed to know the moment we crossed. It came and flew by with no apparent notice. I was now in Ireland. So much of an anticlimax.

Deciding to walk to the hotel from the station, I bumped my roller bag down the streets. Passing over the O'Connell Bridge, I stroll the Aston Quay into the Temple Bar district. Full of bars and cafes I looked forward to an evening here. It looked lively, and the hotel I had booked was right in the middle. I had a meeting set with an Irish Greenkeeper to discuss the future of what our company could do in Ireland, who was doing what, and generally get a good idea of the market. We had met at a previous event, and since I was in NI, it made sense to meet and discuss further in Dublin. We had made a plan to meet at a bar later that evening. All I had to do was find it.

Firstly though I wanted to get a shower, change and grab some food. I arrived at the madly painted Blooms Hotel, where I was given a spotless and well-sized room. The only negative was the view. I had a solid brick wall. And it was not even a beautiful wall. But since the room was filled with fluffy white towels, I did not care at all. The hotel had a restaurant and bar, so I thought it would be perfect for dealing with my hunger.

After dinner, I took a nice walk along the waterfront and around the Temple Bar area. As I mentioned, it is full of pubs offering Guinness to tourists. By this, I mean some are poured with care, and some are not. I had some good and some bad. The good were perfect, and the bad were embarrassing for the venue so I shall not name them here. I had one particularly badly poured Guinness in one of the most well know bars in temple bar. The guy threw the glass near the tap and filled in one go sloshing it around. He could not possibly be Irish. And he also knew he was not pouring for an Irishman either so probably did not care.

I found a spot where it was warm but outside and had a cigarette with my pint. As is with most Irish bars, you start to chat with other people with ease. It is just normal to interact with the people around you immediately. I love this, and the Irish for this persona. I met a son and mother from Birmingham. It was her birthday, and he had booked a trip for his mother with him. Firstly I thought this very weird, but as I got to know them more, it was terrific. They must have a fantastic relationship. I was also to discover that it was her first-ever flight or travel experience out of mainland UK.

Meeting up with the guy I had come to see in the first place we talked turf and fertiliser for a few hours over many pints of Guinness in a selection of bars. He wanted me to see the whole area only to point out that once you have done this bit, you never go back. You have done the tourist route then. He further suggested that while I was in the area, I should go to the Guinness brewery. Now having had a number of them I didn't feel that an early morning trip to a brewery was not the ideal thing to do. But then again I thought it would be a good thing to experience and tick the box of having done it. I had a few hours before my flight back in the morning to London so I agreed that I would do it.

The Guinness brewery was a twenty-minute walk from my hotel. I checked out and left my roller bag in the reception to pick up on my way back. The closer you get to this giant of brewing building, the poorer the place looks. Mixed in with the gambling shops and tobacco shops were, weirdly, several shops selling suits tailor-made for children. Also, there was a grocery shop that had a photo of the inside of the shop on the outside. A way to entice you in they may have hoped. I went in to see if this theory stood up. It did not. The shit looking interior on the picture outside was worse in real life. I bought some water and left.

I purchased tickets on my phone while in the line to go into the brewery. The tour was excellent. I saw all the advertising throughout the ages. The water was displayed in a mesmerising way, flowing through a room down into the brewery rooms I guess. There are things to do if you have time and want to spend more money. You can make a glass, learn to pour a pint and design some sort of advertising thing. I moved further and further up the pint glass-shaped inner building to the 360degree rooftop bar where you are given a pint. Not that I wanted it at 9:30 am. I was a little shaky from the previous evening, and I managed to knock it on a table and spilt half of it over the counter. Embarrassed, I slipped away and left the bar to walk down again through the museum section towards the final stop—the shop. I wanted to buy something but could not for the vast expense most of the items were. I decided on the memory and a few pictures as my souvenir.

Walking back towards the hotel to grab my bag I thought about Dublin and how that this little experience that I had in less than a day has been so brilliantly replicated in almost every city in the world. You know what I mean. You go somewhere, and you will always find an Irish bar. And you will always find friendly people in there where the boundaries of conversation are dropped. It matters not who you are. You are welcome and invited to join in the fun. I guess that is what Ireland is. I do look forward to returning.

Next week it is Italy, Slovenia, and Croatia with the Agronomist. Maybe there are Irish bars there too.

8. Italy, Slovenia, and Croatia March 2019

After a standard Southern Rail delay of my train I meet the Agronomist at Gatwick South Terminal for breakfast. We were off to Ljubljana in Slovenia for a presentation. We found that the most accessible and cheapest option was to fly to Venice and then drive to Slovenia. I had not been to Venice before, so I had suggested that since we had to drive up through the mountains into Slovenia, then down to Croatia the following day, why not drive into the late evening and have a night in Venice instead of a last night in Croatia. We had an early morning flight back to the UK, and this way it meant that we did not have to stress with an early morning four hour drive crossing boarders, finding a fuel station, and dropping off the hire car. He agreed and we looked forward to an evening in Venice.

Over the airport breakfast, we discussed the plane crash in Ethiopia that had recently happened. I had discovered that an old friend was onboard it. Disasters close to home do make you think. I fly a lot as you can work out and it is a numbers game. But this is my job. To be all over Europe, visiting customers and supporting them. And if I looked at the stats in 2017, there were no commercial aircraft disasters at all. So it is still the safest way to travel. It reminds me to get a new life insurance policy in Sweden when we move in July.

I am to move countries this year. I have lived in the UK for only five years, but since I have a Swedish wife and children, we decided that we wished to return to Sweden. It is slightly cheaper to buy a house there, and I quite like the Scandinavian lifestyle.

Anyway, Sitting right at the back on the plane the Agronomist and I checked over our presentations.

Our hire car, a Fiat 500, was a delight. I love these little cars. Not massively powerful but brilliant non the less. Perfect for the small city roads of Italy. We, however, had quite some hours in the thing to spend, crossing into Slovenia and then on to the Croatian coast. But first, we had to fill the back seats and boot with our luggage. It was getting dark when we crossed into Slovenia. The wonderful views of the end of the Alps I had described to the Agronomist were therefore not available to him. It did not matter. We found our way into Ljubljana City centre to find our hotel was not in it. We located the new Radisson Hotel in the outskirts of the city. We parked outside and went to check in with a man who was a spitting image to "Tag" from the sitcom "Friends".

Quite tired and wanting to be fresh for the morning presentation, we go to the hotel restaurant. Now I know that the business hotels chains charge more for their food and beverages than local areas, but when it is almost 300% more, I refuse to oblige. We left the restaurant after looking at the menu and took the €5 taxi ride to the city centre. We are dropped almost on the Dragon Bridge. This magnificent bridge was built-in 1900 to 1901 and the first reinforced concrete structure in Slovenia. Some say that if a virgin crosses the bridge, the tails of the four dragons guarding it on each post move. Not being able to test this, we walked over the bridge in search of food.

We stopped at a few menu posts to check them out. The restaurants all looked a little romantic for us so walking on we discover a collection of three bridges all crossing roughly the same space within meters of each other. Odd. We went over one of them and walked into a place that clearly served cheese and various hams. And wine.

Initially, we sat outside, but as the heaters were superheating our legs and no warmth reached anywhere else, it was not comfortable. Moving inside, we sat on a small table where we could watch the barman in action. It was a little place, quite pleasant with a feeling of true localness. Wines filled the shelves, and various dried meets festooned the bar top, and hanging from the ceiling. There were cheeses too, many of them all on offer to us. And if this is a way or marketing, then it worked. We ordered many.

We choose menu one that offered platters of meat and cheese. Amazing. Oh, I wish I could remember the place to let you, the readers, know where it is. We also shared a delightful wine by the way.

It was so delicious that our second round of meat and cheese came out of our own money. We did not want to push the boundaries of our expense accounts.

After sleeping with my minibar door open to cool down the oven that was my room, I went down to meet up with our Slovenian distributor Uros. He has been working with our company for many years—a great guy with an odd habit of wearing colourful hair bands to keep his hair in check. I keep on having to stop myself from buying a hairband for him with wobbly bits on springs.

He informed us of the days' proceedings and who I might be meeting at the presentation event. We were not the only company presenting, and we looked forward to meeting new people.

The presentations went well with myself and the Agronomist bouncing back and forth of each other presentations. We had much interest and even received an invitation to visit the national stadium while we were there. We made the arrangements and headed out to the national teams training ground for a visit and walkabout. The backdrop of the mountains north of the city is a picture-perfect sight. I took many photos. I have been into the mountains on a private visit with my family, and I highly recommend it. They are indeed a hidden gem in Europe. In fact, I think Slovenia is. Just don't tell anyone.

We arrived at the National Stadium and went into its massive underground car park to meet the head groundsman in his workshop. We met the whole team actually. The place is very impressive, and we had a pleasant walk over the pitch looking and discussing different things. The Chairman came over and asked a few questions to us. He suggested that we go for lunch. Not wanting to be rude, we agreed, and the Chairman then sent us out to a restaurant with the Head Groundsman. We continued our discussions and filled our stomachs with great local produce. Stuffed, we parted company and went back to the hotel with our Uros so pleased that we managed to visit the stadium.

We had planned dinner in the centre of Ljubljana again. I had done a little research into this city, and there was a feature I wanted to explore. I downloaded the app and proceeded to explain to the other two about the water taps of Ljubljana. Both of them were stunned.

"What, you want to visit water taps?" They said.

I explained that all across the city are more than fifty taps all designed oddly and can be visited using an App to direct you. We found a few and then the other two complained that they were cold and wanted a real drink. Uros, the man with the hairband obsession, guided us towards a Slovenian tapas bar and restaurant where he said the food was to be brilliant. It was, and again I forget the name. I should get better at this. Especially if I am trying to combine a travel book with my journal here. I will get better I promise.

The following day we were to meet in Croatia. I had driven this epic road before with my family, and I was looking forward to it very much. The weather was sunny; the Fiat was loaded; we were ready. We drove into the elevator from the car park and went slowly up. Oh yes, I have forgotten to mention this brilliant feature of the Radisson in Ljubljana. It has a car elevator. You drive in it and open the window to choose your floor. Love it. I think it should be standard for all hotels.

I digress again, we head out to the border and arrive in about an hour or so. We leave the Slovenian side all well and then stop at the border of Croatia. The border officer asked us for passports and car documents. We handed him the passports and the rental agreement.

He shouted at us.

"Car Document!"

I said sorry the car is a rental from Italy so I don't have any other documents.

He yells at me.

"Car Document!"

I ask the Agronomist to look in the glove box.

We hand over everything to the guy. Sort of happy he asks

"How long you in Croatia?"

"Three hours" I say.

He almost throws the documents back at me, and we enter Croatia.

We stop for a quick coffee and receive the final location details of where we are to meet Uros. Directions set into the phone we drive on, noticing that almost every house had a small strip of perfectly ploughed land. Not very big, about 3 m long, but the work had defiantly been done by a tractor and plough and not by hand. We wonder if there is a local entrepreneur with a tractor and plough and thought...I can make money with this. Happy thoughts.

We carry on towards the highway windy roads and villages. Many a biker obviously uses the roads in the summertime as we passed a few signs counting down to a spot where all the motorbikes fall over. Well, that is what it looked like to us. It could just be the severity of the bend.

We arrive and meet with Uros at a stadium on the hill in the town of Rijeka. The pitch is the location where in the past England and Croatia had a closed game. Maybe they had issues with their documents too. Anyway, we are asked if we would do an improvised presentation. We agreed and since we had the presentation from the day before we just repeated that. This time we were not in a hotel conference room. We were in the pressroom where the team managers talk about the game before and after. It felt odd but brilliant at the same time.

We had one more stadium to visit while on our short trip to Croatia. This one was to be literally on the waterfront to the Adriatic Sea. Certainly one of the most distinct football pitches in the world. They had used our products for a while now, and we're pleased to have our visit to see how things were going. We made some suggestions and talked with the whole team there.

It was soon time to take the long drive back to Venice Airport, where we were to drop the car off. Before the Agronomist and I left, we grabbed some very late lunch and recapped the overall trip and made further plans for following up all that we had set in motion.

The drive back was boring and with no issue at all. Even the borders were nothing to write about. We just went through.

After another uninteresting period of time that included dropping the car off at the airport, we went in search of the bus to take us across to the island of Venice. There are options directly from the airport to take you by boat but since I don't do boats I insisted we went by road.

The main terminal on the island which consists of the car parks, the bus and train station, is a busy and an utterly confusing place. It is a large square where there are numerous maps to get you even more confused.

On the basis we had our phones we just plugged in the hotel address and went for it. Thirty minutes walk apparently! Great! My roller bag will have some great fun bouncing on the cobbled streets of this ancient and sinking city. I also had the pop-up stand to carry too, which was also not in the least uncomfortable to carry. Finally, after only getting lost once, we reached our hotel on the opposite side of the city. On the way, we did see some of the exciting tourist sights including the bridge over the grand canal and the tower in the square, but we wanted to get a sunset drink in before we went on a real walkabout.

Making it just as we see the sun dipping, we hastily launch our bags into the rooms and head for the outside waterfront bar. Two wines arrive, and we sit in silence, watching and absorbing the spectacular sight.

The streets are narrow and filled with up-and-over stairs passing rather smelly canals. I can't imagine how it must stink in the summer. With all those tourists I feel very sorry for the local residents. And there are many tourists, indeed. We walked around, and I looked at a few masks. I had been keen to get one for my shelf of shit but could not decide between the real Casanova style or some other one with the long penis looking nose. Anyway, we eventually arrived at the bridge over the grand canal. And what a bridge it is. One of the most photographed bridges in the world, I guess. The sunset was magnificent and shone over the buildings to the sides of the canal. We took many pictures of it and other tourists.

Feeling a bit hungry and in need of some wine, we walked into the first restaurant with a canal-side seat available. I started to feel seasick just looking at the gondolas bobbing up and down on what is a bustling canal.

After a pizza and a good hour of people watching, we decided to head off to one of the bars that I had found on an app. It suggested an excellent cocktail bar that Hemingway frequented on his travels here. There was never going to be a good reason to come again as there is very little turf on the island. So we may as well see as much as we could.

We walked right into this bar and then, realising we were very much underdressed and certainly would not have the intellect to converse, we walked right out again. Luckily enough around the corner was a brightly lit bar called Bra Bar. There was sufficient space for us at the bar, and we ordered drinks. Shortly after ordering, we noticed the hundreds of bras hanging from the roof. Quite odd for this place, we thought. Anyhow, it was almost 11 o'clock, and we were now on the opposite side of the island to where the hotel was. We headed out on our way back and bumped into a group of people chatting and drinking. Enjoying the conversation and their wine, I noticed the Agronomist had disappeared.

Venice is not a place to get drunk in. You could easily fall in one of the hundreds of canals, and nobody would ever know. I mean at one point the Agronomist got a wet foot by walking into the canal. Not wanting to embarrass him further, I shall leave that story alone.

I awoke early and took my iPad out to my balcony. The first time this year it was a nice temperature to enjoy sitting outside with a coffee and work in the early morning sunshine. A perfect end to the trip. We prepared ourselves for the long walk back to catch the bus to the airport only stopping for me to buy a mask and to prevent the loud noise coming from my bag bouncing on the cobbles.

On the plane, we had a last view of Venice before heading inland and over the Alps and homeward bound.

With a few weeks away from the trepidations of travel, and being based at home, I was looking forward to having family time. The next trip was to be a personal one to Sweden on an airline I may have a rant about.

9. Sweden March 2019

We were on a private trip to Sweden, to do a spot of house hunting, my wife Lina, and I wanted to go as cheap as we possibly could. So Lina booked us a flight on an airline that likes the colour yellow. It was cheap. And it flew into an airport that was not Stockholm even though it plays on being one of Stockholms airports. But was closer to where we wanted to be. The only positive bit to the flight.

As I said Lina booked the flights. I had refused to book, go on the website, hand over my credit card details, or email address. I wanted nothing to do with them.

They were cheap, as I have mentioned, and thus in times of saving for the house, I bit my tongue and accepted it.

Lina had booked one priority ticket and one not. We only needed one large carry on bag for the few nights stay, so that was fine. We both had our small onboard bags for iPad and headphones etc.

I thought I would download the app and get the check-in done. While putting in the passport details I immediately started shouting at the phone app. It kept on suggesting that I should book a seat for as little as £4. There was no seat that I could find for £4, so I decided not to bother and gave up.

After calming down I finally checked us in, and they put us so far away from each other it was stupid. Just because I refuse to pay for a seat two people on the same booking code must be placed at opposite sides of the plane why?How desperate are you for the customer to book and pay for seats to want that?

Now I travel quite a lot, and I do understand that people go on holidays and then that is it for the year. It is a novelty, and airports for these people are a luxury shopping mall. But you must have some kind of idea that when you go through security that you must remove your coins, your keys and a half litre of coke. And then we find the phone in the back pocket, and then the bag needs to have all the vodka removed from it together with the laptop you did not take out even after seeing sixteen signs and hearing the security office should out in advance. Got this makes me angry.

Anyway breathe, I am on a cheap trip to save money, and I must also remember that I am certainly not flying out of one of London's only two real airports.

Boarding this sort of airline, your fingered out if you have not paid for anything other than the airfare. You stand while most of the passengers get in the priority queue where they can waft down with their two bags and widely printed out "priority" boarding passes. Never try to jump as you will be told you are in the wrong line and are not a priority to the staff. Get to the back you low life is the tone.

When it was the time for the non-priority passengers to have their bags checked for size and then forced to pay £20 on the spot for each extra bag they had no priority to have, the escalator down to the boarding section was turned off. We, the non-priority people, are told to use the stairs.

I board from the rear of the plane, naturally, as this is what happened to slaves back in the day. You know where your standing is. I found my brightly coloured seat and hunted for a small netting section in the seat in front of me to put my iPad, water, and magazine. There wasn't one. I then thought I would hang my jacket on the little hook on the side of the seat in front as you get on most other airlines. There was not one of those either. Well, as I type all the above belongings except for the iPad are on the floor set up as trip obstacles in the unlikely chance there is an emergency.

Oh, and another thing. The steward came on and suggested that we could have breakfast or indeed lunch, both of which consisted of ham and cheese stuck inside something delicious. I doubted that very much. Ham and cheese put in bread, a croissant or anything is not delicious when warmed up in the microwave. It is a cure for a hangover, end. I was going to get a coffee, but I am not now for fear of being told that I don't have priority enough for a spoon.

My wife and I had had an excellent trip to Sweden, and everything had gone according to plan with the house seen, and the bank managers agreement to give us a mortgage.

And so I thought it was over with my rant, but it is not.

On our return, I experience my first bit of irritation at the security when we were told that our bag was precisely 11kg and not the 10kg we were allowed. They let us through but with some reluctance. We went on to security. Now security is usually fine. I mean the people managing the security have, in my opinion, one of the most critical jobs at an airport. They give everyone who has passed a sense of...well security.

Now on every one of the flights I have taken over the past ten years, I have taken my Zippo Lighter with me. Well, I now only have the outside of it as they took the middle bit away from me. With not so much to do about it I mumble irritating comments that embarrassed Lina and packed my stuff and went upstairs to the smoking room. I had got some emergency matches in my bag that they had not taken away from me.

This time Lina joined me in the non-priority queue, and we boarded the not so busy flight. We went to our seats and found out that I, being non-priority, was rammed between two other people and my wife, being priority having two free places next to her. I asked to move, and the stewardess let me move to sit next to her—something I did not expect at all.

With only a slight delay, we take-off. And soon the chips and ham and cheese sandwiches came rolling down the aisle. Not drinks, you must wait for them; first, they want you to part with ten euros for a box of hot chips.

Anyway, I opened my chocolate protein bar and drank my water adamantly not ever wanting to give any of my money to this airline again. I will pay for a "normal airline" and long to be treated as an adult and not a child. End of Rant.

10. Portugal April 2019

After a few weeks of being based at home, except for a few overnight stays for UK sales meetings, I am back on board a British Airways A320 on my way to the Algarve, in Portugal.

I am not complaining at all. I have never been to this part of Portugal, and since I shall be personally mobile with a hire car, I am looking forward to zipping around some great golf courses and meeting some great new people. It is part of my job that I look forward to, new places, new friendships, and hopefully new business.

The flight in was brilliant, a great view of the coast on the approach to Faro airport. The speed in which you go through passport and baggage is like no other of similar size.

I walk out and onwards to the exit to have a smoke. I then find that I have to walk back through a segregated section of the airport to collect my hire car. After the usual sales pitch of insurance and other things, you are generally covered for; I pick up my untouched car. The paperwork suggested that it had no previous scratches or marks whatsoever. Since my issue in Norway with the micro scratch, I always check the vehicle over.

Oh My God, what a collection of marks and scratches. Wheels, both rearview mirrors, the front splitter, the rear, the side doors. I promptly found a person to go through with me and mark up all the issues. If I had not done anything that would have been a massive bill for my insurance company. Not entirely sure the excuse of "the system had not been updated" I believe. Undoubtedly a top tip I can offer you for nothing. Always check your hire car.

The Hotel golf resort was only 25 minutes away, so I thought it wise to drive over and check-in before heading to the university where the seminar that I was to attend was.

So after sitting for an hour listening to two presentations in Portuguese, I made my arrangements to meet with a greenkeeper at the hotel I was staying and left. I had already made some prior arrangements with Joel, at time of writing, the President of the Portuguese Greenkeepers Association the following morning which was my main aim of this trip, and since he is also the course manager at magnificent parklands and links golf course about 45 minutes up the coast, I wanted to visit him there. I had first met Joel in Rome at the Federation of European Golf Greenkeepers event.

And what a golf course it turned out to be. The views are amazing. And the properties surrounding it are out of this world.

After a very informative meeting, I left the club and thought I would visit the two "big" names in golf on the Algarve. Quinta Do Lago and San Lorenzo golf clubs.

What an entrance to these clubs, or rather the estates that they are situated. I thought that my morning visit was an expression of property wealth, but this place is another level. This is the Wentworth of the Algarve. Feeling a little misplaced, I walk around, pick up some useful information from the Greenkeepers and went back to my more modest golf course resort hotel.

I do love this place and look forward to launching the company brand here. Just need to check with the big boss that my next few visits can be authorised. So If I am back later in this book with a trip to the Algarve you know, I got the go-ahead. All part of my new role,

I guess.

Anyhow, one last important meeting to do before I leave, and that is to meet up with Lee, whom I had also not seen since I was at the FEGGA (Federation of European Golf Greenkeepers Association) gathering in Rome a few chapters back. Being not in competition to us, but having the same area to cover it is always lovely to meet a friendly face. He is also half Portuguese, so that helps too.

Getting picked up at precisely 7 pm by the Lee and his dealer, a guy called Toni, we quickly zoom off to a bar called the *Fat Frog* where we met with a Danish contractor who has been in the region for more than 35 years. Toni had also been in the region for more than 40 years and it was nice to meet locals.

In the *Fat Frog*, we drank many small beers as we talked about work, life and all things between. The Frog, apparently, keeps the gipsies away. Bad luck or something so they would not enter the bar.

We talk and drink late into the night. I recall getting back very late and felt suitably in pain the following day. But having these evenings to understand the market, the place, and what is needed to gain business is vitally important.

Having dropped the hire car off, I went straight through security in the priority lane right to the front of the line. This annoyed one gentleman, and he had to be informed by a security man that I was not rude as he was shouting out, but just had more priority than him in this situation. A bit like how I felt on my recent trip to Sweden.

I bought a tomato juice in the departure lounge and waited for the flight to board. It had been a great trip, and I look forward to my next visit if I get the go-ahead.

Now it is a Friday, and I have downloaded the latest Grand Tour to watch on this flight. Next trip is to Austria. So until then.

11. Austria April 2019

I have managed to get a few days trip to Vienna and the surrounding golf courses there. Directly after the Easter Bank Holiday, I am up for a 4:30 am Taxi to go to Heathrow.

Having slept almost all the taxi ride to Terminal 3, I head straight for the lounge and a coffee. This lounge was a new one for me. Called the *Aspire Lounge* it is open for anyone if you pay your £20. The lounge is small, quiet and, fitted with a bar and more importantly sleeping pods. These are different and quite comfortable. After breakfast, I spent fifteen moments of shut-eye and then it was time to head to the gate.

My hire car on this occasion was a Peugeot 208, now I don't want to sound like Clarkson or any of the trio, but it was powerless, and the gearbox area heated up so much that after a modest half-hour drive my leg was on fire. There were more pockets and useless storage sections than necessary. If I emptied my satchel, I would still have little spaces that needed filling.

My hotel, The Austria Trend, chosen simply for the price, was situated a fifteen-minute drive or a forty-five-minute walk from the centre of Vienna. Right next to one of the highways. This was convenient for getting out and about to my customers as no need for sitting in traffic, and close enough you could grab the tram line into the city. Or walk. Since this was mostly a travel day, I spent the afternoon catching up with emails and planning for the forthcoming week in Norway. At beer 0'clock, I wandered down to the reception. It was then that I discovered that the hotel did not serve evening meals. It was raining outside, and I asked if there anything close by to grab some dinner. They had recommended the Irish Bar 300 m from the hotel. With this new knowledge I cancel the drink order and went there for an Irish pint instead. As I have mentioned before, I find Irish bars are perfect for meeting people. You are never alone in one for long.

I love Irish bars. Dingy, dark, generally full of ex-pats, and you know exactly what to expect. In fact, on my walk, I decided what I was going to have for dinner: a steak and Guinness pie.

They served it up with a beautiful pint, and I chatted to the chef and some bar staff over a full second pint and then went back to the hotel to watch rubbish on my iPad.

After a full day of visiting five golf courses and drinking far too much coffee and with a proper 25000 steps accomplished, I park up at my hotel. It is 29 Degrees, and I require a shower and refresh.

At about 5 O'clock I walk into the city. A pleasant 30-minute walk it turned out. I passed the Jardin du Bélvedère and popped in to have a quick look at what I had been informed by a customer was a most beautiful garden. They were not lying it is and with a view of the 18th-century old castle. It is free and open to walk around, and many people were undoubtedly enjoying the evening with ice cream amongst the shrubberies.

Moving further towards the city centre, I come across The Hochstralbrunnen. It is a multi statue with multicoloured lights that shine up the water as it is blasted up. It has been around since 1873, but I am sure the lighting was an addition many years after. I study it for a while and then tackle the road crossing towards the centre of the Vienna.

I had been given some suggestions for bars to visit in the city by one of the ex-pat Greenkeepers I met earlier in the day. Albeit he recommended only ex-pat bars. One, in particular, they all end up in when they are in the city themselves—*Flanagan's Irish Bar*. Oh well, I could do with a pint, and it was only a few minutes walk away.

With a drink in front of me, I decide to grab some food. So far this trip I have eaten two nights in one of the most diverse cities in Europe and both have been a pint of Guinness and non-local food. I must stop this, I said to myself. Thankfully I was not in control of the next night as I was to meet with the President of the Greenkeepers Association of Austria and he had arranged everything.

I walk back with a few diversions from my original route, and finally, an hour later, I reach the hotel. Another shower and I am in bed by 11 pm. Not a bad day with almost 40,000 Steps accomplished according to my gizmo.

I visit two more courses—both of them a good hour away from the city north of the Danube. I enjoy driving through this region, just north-east of Vienna, I had crossed the river twice and followed its shoreline for a while. It is flat here, with long vast views of fields of strawberries and then in the distant, and you get a view of the mountains.

After the two meetings, I drove back towards the city. I decided to take a different route as I had wanted for a while now to visit the snow globe museum. The museum is situated on the opposite side of the city to my hotel, but since I was driving from that direction, I took the detour. Did you know that Vienna was the home of Snow Globes? Me neither, but it is, and you can get whatever you bring put in one. I had brought with me a small matchbox Land Rover Defender. Being a bit of a Landy fan, and owner, I wanted to have one on my desk.

Anyway, it was closed. Next time maybe.

The evening I was to meet with the President of the Austrian Greenkeepers association as I have mentioned before. He sent me the address and name of the meeting spot. It was called *Wine and Co.* Simply a wine bar with food and a shop. Interesting I thought, and they certainly have a good selection of wine from all over the world. But we were here to taste Austrian wine. Something I don't often drink. It was a good evening, and I learned many things about Austrian wine and the producing areas and vineyards.

After the wine and excellent food, we parted company, and I took a taxi back, but my wine-infused brain said to stop at *O'Connells*, the Irish bar for a beer. It was close to the hotel, and since it was not even 10 pm I thought, why not?

I immediately met up with the chef again that served me on the first night in the bar. We had a beer and then a very drunk Costa Rican girl with no bra arrived into the bar. She continued to get more drunk with a police officer, who was also under the influence. I could not leave this. It was too funny to miss. And she had no bra.

Next to the policeman, was a guy who can only be described as being a hells angels representative. They had some amusing banter at the bar and seam to have got on well. The Hells Angels rep left after swapping numbers with the policeman, and all was fine. The Costa Rican girl was still on full form swaying from side to side and certainly looked like she was very interested in the policeman.

Probably about half an hour after the Hells Angels guy had left, he burst back into the bar all angry and shouting. What had transpired was that the policeman had given his new best friend his number with a heart on the note next to it. This did not go down well. Oozing with manhood, it got heated, and the guys started to get more and more heated. Each accusing the other of being homosexual or homophobic and each of them did not like the other's opinions being pushed on them by the other.

I have to admit I did think at one point that I would be involved in a blocking capacity. Not that I think I would last more than a second. Either one of these guys would have knocked me to the ground in a heartbeat; still, it was funny. The pretty Hungarian barmaid dealt with the situation swiftly and professionally.

The policeman eventually staggered out, and I had a lock-in with the manager, the Pretty Hungarian and the drunk Costa Rican, Sometimes I look back at these moments, and I think that I cant make this shit up. I blame the Irish bar culture.

My last day In Vienna and I have lots of emails to catch up with before I meet up with the majority of the ex-pat greenkeepers for their "Peaky Blinders Golf Society" Golf day. I try to attend as many as possible as it is so much fun and a great way to meet the guys who are not just head Greenkeepers but all the guys whom you never know where they will end up. It is all about networking.

I arrive at the club, pick up my borrowed clubs, take the traditional photo and embarrass myself with losing two balls off the first tee out of bounds. I did play quite ok after that but not wanting to go into my golf round in this book let's just say I ended up average.

With a late afternoon flight, I had to make my excuses and hit the highway to the airport. I had used some points to upgrade myself, so I could have dinner on-board and gain the tier points needed to keep my Silver-tier on BA. The extra points were the only reason actually as the meal was crap. What I will say is that I do like the new touch that BA do with your name when asking what drink you want. Still, there is no real reason to fly any other way than economy within Europe.

Next week, a full week away in Norway.

12. Norway April/May 2019

Arriving at Heathrow, I checked in my luggage for free as the flight was to be full and headed for security and the *Prestige lounge.* I had noticed it on previous visits to Heathrow while boarding at gate A5, where the entrance to the lounge is situated. I had also noticed that it had an American Express sign. I thought that I would try it out and see if the Platinum card I possess would get me in for free. It did. Happy, I went directly to the breakfast buffet and helped myself to much of it. This was made even more brilliant as directly above this lounge is the BA Galleries lounge. Which if you gain Silver membership you get to have a dry bacon bap. Here I don't have to do anything and have a full English and fruit selection for free. Feeling smug, I indulged and read the news over my breakfast and occasionally looking up to all the business people in the BA lounge eating their horrid bacon roll.

My Hire car in Norway was a Ford Focus estate. Now there is something about all Fords that make them fun to drive. I would never in a million years own one, but I do like driving them. And I needed this upgrade as I was to be loading and delivering some products to customers that arrived late to Norway on a previous order.

First stop, however, was a long drive to almost the end of one of the arms of the Oslo fjord. A great track of a golf course and my first time visiting it. I had met Logan, the course manager many times before at either events or in Oslo city. His account had been handed over to me by a colleague, and I thought it best to visit the course to get an idea of where he was located.

On my way back to Oslo city, I had to stop by the warehouse where a pallet of fertiliser had been delivered for me to pick up. I called ahead and discovered that it was going to be closed at 3 pm. It was 2:45 pm, and I was never going to make it. Being unhelpful, they did not want to wait for 15 minutes for me. So I asked what time they opened. 6 am they informed me. I said I would be there when they opened as I had to pick the items up to deliver over the coming days. Slightly irritated with the diversion I had to make the following morning, I headed for my overnight stop.

I had booked the hotel in central Oslo. I like being in this city. There is much to do and getting around is very easy on foot. The Scream, by Edvard Munch, is worth a visit. By the time this book will be published, it will be housed in its modern building next to the opera house on the Oslo Fjord. The walk to the roof of the opera house is a must also—a particularly special spot to view the city. You walk from the waters edge up the slope on one side and then make a turn and carry on until you are on the roof. A fantastic bit of architecture, I must say. And an exceptional addition to the city of cool buildings.

I had not stayed in this hotel before, but I was gaining points, so I did not care. The parking was close, and although expensive, it is secure and out of the weather.

That night I simply grabbed a meal in a restaurant opposite the hotel—a nothing special place offering pizza. The hotel did not have any restaurant itself as it was cheap. Just a cafe where breakfast was to be served. Not that I was going to get any the next day. While people-watching over my pizza I spot an Irish bar so, with a weak mind I went there for an after-dinner Guinness. There was live music, and it was ok, not brilliant by the usual Irish bar standards. But it was a Monday.

The warehouse was a simple place to get to. The main highway south out of the city and head towards the town of Drammen. I arrive and am met by a large man sitting outside in the sun with his morning coffee. He sorted the paperwork for me. Kindly, he moved the pallet reasonably close to the car and then sat down and watched me move 325 kg of our stock into the vehicle. Not an inkling of help. Sweating I took a call from the big boss of the company I work for and finished the job off.

Now in my low riding hire car, I swiftly drove toward the first customer. He was to take most of the weight out of the car, so a priority for me. The road was light, unlike me. I drove for the first time through the tunnel under the Oslo fjord. With a speed limit of 50kph and the gradient steep, all the traffic becomes forced to sit on their breaks. So deep under the fjord, it smells like burning brakes. Going up, I struggled a bit I have to say. I have no idea what size the engine was in my Ford, but not a lot was my guessing. But I made it. And after I delivered most of the goods at the first-course visit of the day, I sat with the course manager Steve and enjoyed a robust Norwegian coffee. He had been in Norway for several years and thus had developed the most Norwegian taste for coffee. Basically treacle in a cup.

Second on my visits was one of the first customers I ever had in Norway. I arrived early and met with Duncan, John, and Johns dog Luna, who guards the workshop with her vicious sounding bark and her waggly fluff tail.

We always have good banter when at this club. Duncan had recently purchased a new car. A hybrid. And his super kind colleagues had painted his new parking place near the workshop with a marking that could be interpreted as inappropriate, so I shall not go into detail here.

Out on the golf course again although this time we were trying to locate the extent of massive beaver damage. The little critters had been very busy. And ambitious. A huge tree was very close to being toppled close to a green. It needed dealing with before any accident could happen. So with the course looking spectacular, I said my goodbyes and moved on.

My final visit of the day is a golf course at a school. This nine-hole track has been the discussion point of Oslo for the past few years. Nobody knows how long it will still be there for. Yet the course greens looked great coming out of the winter and hats off to the course manager, Gavin, for doing a good job there.

Driving back to Oslo, the traffic was starting to build up. I had forgotten it was a bank holiday the following day and that means only one thing in Norway. Half-day previous to it is also off. Thankfully I was heading into town and against the traffic.

Now I know Oslo pretty well to walk around but not to drive. It has continuously changed its one way system and trams only lanes over the past few years, and it can be very confusing. There is no way to understand it. I spent at least 15 mins trying to get from one side of the city to the other. I could almost see where I wanted to be but could not get there. Eventually, I drove back out and came at from another angle, that seemed to work as I found the car park quite easily this time.

Before grabbing a shower, I sent in my complex expenses form on my new app. It was not confusing at all. Sorry to digress but I have been testing out a new app for all the receipts I gain while travelling and I get quite a bit. Not an easy task, but it all needs to be allocated in the system somehow to each of the countries I visit. Anyway, I was late and made a mess of it. So got a telling off, rightly so. I promised everyone and myself that I would sort it for the next month. There is not too much paperwork in this job, but expenses are the one thing you need to get right.

Anyhow, after my rejuvenating shower, I decided to go to a restaurant I know to have some whale. You may have your opinions on this, but I love it. You get a small taster dish followed by an amazing pork knuckle. This with a local brew is all that is needed and by Norway prices it is very cheap.

I went back to the hotel, and my sauna(room) was still up to top temp. I could not open the window as there was a football game going on live in the bar opposite. It was so loud and hot I considered putting my pillow inside the minibar and sleeping there, but instead, I got dressed, and I popped into the Irish bar for a nightcap and then back to the hotel to watch some crap on the iPad I had downloaded. The music was still loud, but I opened up the windows anyway, put my noise-cancelling headphones on and went to sleep.

The morning started slowly. I had experienced a rubbish sleep as the noise from the bar outside my room did not shut up until 3 am, but then it was quiet. Being a bank holiday in Norway, the streets are deserted early in the morning. I had breakfast and walked down the road through a full brass band towards the car park.

Norway really does celebrate their holidays. Nobody works. And the May Day bank holiday is full of brass bands and marches through the city centre. Well, I had a job to do, and that was another hour drive down to a golf course managed in consultation by James, a course manager of another course. He had recently taken over the role here, and I had a full tour of each hole. Backwards not to annoy the golfers. It was also a new customer, so it was great to see the place for the first time.

At one point we were driving towards a bridge that had quite damaged sidewalls. It had clearly been hit by numerous club cars and other machines in the past. But as I was in mid-sentence to point this out, James hit the side of the bridge with the front wheel. I burst into laughter and promised to tell everyone. We reversed and went another way around the course.

On my way back into Oslo city I found the car park in one go. I was pleased with my navigation skills. I went to my room and finished off some paperwork. I decided to have an early evening walk down to the Ake Brygge part of Oslo. It was packed full of people enjoying the sun of the bank holiday.

Ake Brygge is a part of Oslo I like. It is more expensive than most, so I tend not to eat here but it well worth the people watching. I had a beer in the sun and relaxed.

After a terrible dinner, I remembered that my hotel was to have a bar opening for the first time on this day. I hurried back to enjoy the opening. On my arrival to the reception and bar area I see that they had two bottles of red and two bottles of white. The atmosphere was like sitting in the reception chairs at a hotel. This is because the seating area is the chairs in the reception of the hotel.

I asked to take my glass up to my room. The receptionist, and now promoted barmaid informed me that having no licence for that I must only drink it in the reception. I did not have a glass of wine. Not sure how popular their bar will be.

Checking out of the hotel for my long day in the car, I managed to forget the pork pies and cheese I had brought for my customers. I do this quite a bit. Not leave them in hotels but bring them. Having been an ex-pat much of my life, I know how much a little taste of home is appreciated. Cheddar cheese, sweets, and pork pies are always a hit.

I visit the first two golf clubs that are next to each other; both managed by Scots. One, Johnny, had been a customer for several years, and the other is a new one and had been testing us on nine holes of the twenty-seven he manages.

It is always about the relationship with the customer. Many of the companies in this industry can supply the result but in a slightly different way. It is down to support and trust in the salesperson. Well, this is my experience anyway.

Leaving these two clubs, I head north to my last visit of the day. A good 4 hour drive away. You can never get bored of the roads there.

Driving through massive fjords and breathtaking views of mountains is just a treat and I often mutter to myself whilst driving how lucky I am to have such a job.

The golf course I visit near the ski area of Hemsedal is unique. It has some of the most brilliant holes around. The whole place is within a residential area of summer/winter cottages. All set with the backdrop of a 100 m waterfall and snow-capped mountains. It is just brilliant.

With the meeting and planning for the year over, I head back towards Honefoss and to stay with Ian, another customer of mine.

I have mentioned him before, we occasionally have a whisky evening with some of his friends, well my friends now too. I do look forward to it. The only time I drink the golden stuff. I am always welcomed with a home-cooked meal by his wife and love to see his children. Such a great family and I thank them for their excellent hospitality every time I am in Norway.

With a slightly heavy head after our whisky tasting, we head together to his golf course where we meet up with his deputy Nick and go through new products and their order for the coming year. To see how things have gone so far coming out of the winter, we head out for a cold course drive. It certainly clears the head.

Having to shoot off for a final course visit near the airport I leave for the drive that takes me north of the city. Unfortunately, I get stuck in a tunnel as there is an accident which causes me to have to cancel my final visit.

When I get to the airport, I check-in and find that SAS had upgraded me to their business section. Cool. I can have the opportunity to check out the SAS lounge. I find it is separated, business and Gold. The gold members have a separate section. I wonder what they get as I help myself to an excellent salad buffet and a glass of wine.

Onboard I am treated to a cube of food and a free drink. Within the cube is neatly placed cutlery and an odd-looking sachet of something dried. I read that they are carrots. But I could not see where the moisture could come from to make them look like carrots. I take them home as a souvenir.

Homeward bound in my taxi looking forward to the UK bank holiday.

It would give me time to prepare for a few days in Portugal, a new country to establish, and I looked forward to the challenge.

13. Portugal May 2019

With a painless train trip to Gatwick airport, I am on my way back to Portugal.

The boss said, yes!

This trip I am to meet a potential new distributor. A person that I have been introduced indirectly by Lee. We have made arrangements to meet in the hotel resort that I stayed in on the previous visit. This time the weather is better, and the flights are more jammed with tourists.

You know that a mid-May flight to the Algarve will have a particular type of person on board. They will already be orange from fake tanning, and the women will generally be wearing some animal pattern on their baggy trouser skirt dress thing, whilst the men will be wearing a football supporters top of some kind. There were two middle-aged women on their way for a golfing break for a week away from their men. And a little bit of "fun" as I overheard. Ordering "bubbles" they got right into the mood.

The car that I had booked was another dribble of rubbish—an Opel. "New" with " no scratches," they said, so as it is in Portugal you check and bring the man over to make notes of the scratches it does have. Since the excess was 3000 Euros, you think of this. All I am doing is helping American Express out as they would have to pick up the bill.

I went directly to my meeting at the hotel complex that I had stayed on my previous visit. After a good meeting with our now new distributor, we decide to go ahead and roll out our brand, offering support as much as we can with several visits during the year.

There was another reason that I had picked this venue too as the meeting spot. During my last visit, I had left my Swedish ID card in the slot for electricity in the room. They kindly had kept it for me until now. I have deposited many cards in these things, mostly credit cards or food supermarket point cards. All easily replaced. But the Swedish ID card would have meant going to the Police Station in Sweden to get a new one which would be a pain.

I noticed as I came down to the lobby that there was some big football match on the television so I thought I would grab a meal away from the noise. Walking around the Vilamoura waterfront, it was quite busy with people. As with many holiday hotspots, waiters were standing near the entrance to their restaurants trying to entice into their restaurant passers-by offering free cocktails or alike. I decided upon a pizza place and devoured a sizeable spicy meat variant washed down with an equally large beer.

One was in bed early but woken with the sound of cheers from the various bars as the football supporters celebrated a score. At 11 pm it was a little annoying. I went back to sleep and woke up at 5:30. I had to leave for a gathering of Greenkeepers to play my first golf competition with them. The Greenkeepers Association of Portugal arranged it, and the chairman invited me to join in and use the game to meet some potential customers.

On the drive, I put the radio on. I had not changed the station in the car as it was a station that played music I liked. However, this morning we had a presenter called Ole, and his program was on "intelligent love". The days' advice was on the reason why men change when they have been in a relationship or moved in together with their "conquest". I am not sure he would not have been on the airwaves for very long in the UK before being shut down and sacked.

Arriving at the club, I was praying that I would not make a fool of myself off the first tee as everyone was standing to wait their turn. I was a little late as I wanted to call home and wish my boys a happy birthday before they went to school. Stressed but ready I teed off and hit a blinder of a drive right down the middle. It was to be the second-best shot of the day for me.

The game was enjoyable, and I met many new faces and potential customers. During the prize-giving and following presentations, Lina called me over and over again. This never happens. It must be important, and I became worried and wished the guy would finish so I could sneak out and call her back. We speak daily, and she never repeatedly calls. Something must be wrong.

Finally outside and on the phone, I ask if the kids were alright, she said that they were but am I sitting down.

What had transpired was that she had gone the end of the driveway where our beloved Land Rover Defender was parked and just as she clicked the remote to unlock it, she noticed it had no doors. And then she saw it had no front seats or bonnet! Some horrible people had stolen these items the previous night. My pride and joy Defender had had its arms and legs pulled off.

I gave her the insurance information for her to register it with the police and went back in to collect my Nearest to the Pin Prize. I can't remember what it was, but I know I drank it when I got back to the hotel that evening whilst putting up notices on various social media platforms and groups about the theft.

I discovered that ours was not the only one; Eight had been targeted that evening it turned out. But we were the only ones not to have the insurance cover the bill. So still at the time of writing, I have my Defender in storage awaiting for me to fit the parts back so

I can drive it once more.

After a refresh I walk towards the restaurant I was to meet Toni. I was early so I turned left into an Irish bar full of British people. They were awaiting another football match to start and their sunburnt bodies to cool. After a pint, I walk to the meeting point. This was a very nice little restaurant, run by a South African. After consuming my swordfish with some delicious wine, we decide to hit a bar, which ended late.

My return flight was at lunchtime, so the morning was set aside for emails and correspondence. Having packed up I headed for a final meeting before reaching the airport with a slightly dizzy head.

Ten minutes into my stay at the BA lounge at Faro Airport, I am called up to speak on the phone to somebody from BA. Puzzled and wondering what I had done, I lifted the receiver and was informed that I had no catering onboard the flight. They had miscalculated it, and I was the only one who would miss out, I would be given some Airmiles. It was fine. I had eaten and not that bothered anyway.

Onboard the head stewardess also informed me again that I had no food allocated to me and would I like to have some extra air miles. I said yes, as I use them to upgrade my return home flights often. You get more points to the collection, and in turn, it makes the next level on the reward program achievable. Plus you get free drinks.

My schedule leaves me in the UK for the coming few weeks. Next overseas would be Italy. And the city of Padua, which will be very interesting. An underrated city in my opinion.

14. Italy May 2019

A plane to Venice from Gatwick airport on a Bank Holiday week-end is always going to be busy. It is rammed with people in flip flops going on a package holiday. I slip into my bubble of noise-cancelling headphones.

I have a couple sitting next to me that have clearly been looking forward to this for some time. The lady has even got dressed up for it. And not to want to sound snobbish, she really could not pull it off especially when her husband has not bothered in the slightest to try to equal her. He still looked like he just go out of bed. Anyway, the drinks trolly arrives at our seat and being first of the economy seats. I look forward to ordering a cup of hot brown.

The lady next to me quietly, but in the poshest accent she can, speaks to the stewardess;

"I know it's far too early. But could I have two gin and tonics please?"

"Absolutely madam, anything for you sir?" She replies.

"Coke, full fat and no ice" He grunts.

As soon as the stewardess moved on the woman speaks to her husband quietly, now back in her standard accent;

"Do you think I should have ordered some bubbles too?"

"Not at that price, Luv!" He huffs and grabs two bags of crisps out of his bag.

Now I have no issue with people bringing onboard snacks. It is essentially saving money, and there is nothing wrong with that. But there are several smells, or should I say flavours that should be banned. Scampi Fries would be one. I like them very much but would not even dream of rustling open a packed on a confined and busy aeroplane. Prawn cocktail flavour should not be allowed either, but that is what they had. She devoured them so fast that the smell thankfully left us about halfway over Spain.

The car hire desk was even busier. I waited for a full hour. I had gone cheap, and with no priority line option, I just listened to my audiobook. I wanted to get to the hotel as fast as possible. Being a Sunday, the Grand Prix was on and one of my favourite ones too, The Monaco Grand Prix.

Finally getting to the hotel, I check-in, order two beers and some nuts and head to my room just in time for David Coulthard to walk the grid. Even on my rushed way to my room, I had noticed that there were three hotels in the complex and that the one I was in was certainly looking a little tired. Still, the sun was out, the outdoor pool looked inviting, and I was totally up for a Sunday afternoon of enjoyment and relaxation watching racing cars fly around Monaco.

After the epic race, I went for a wander. The hotel was a kind of spa retreat. Many people were walking around in robes and those flip flop style white slippers that last precisely the length of your hotel stay. I wandered into the spa area to have a look. I often go for a swim if the hotel I am staying at has a pool. And I enjoy a sauna and steam room, so I went in search of these facilities.

I am told by the receptionist that the entrance to the spa, if I was wearing regular clothes, was down a corridor near the elevators. I entered the corridor and am immediately reminded of a torture scene in some movie I cant remember the name of. Each room was half lit and with the door just ajar enough for me to see what sort of pain should be endured within. There was one room with a stone type of bath and next to it some electronic machine. Electric torture I guessed in there. The next had a machine with pipes and a table with bed combined. Colonic irrigation maybe. I sped up not to get pulled into any room and burst into the light outside and into a rather lovely little cafe/bar by the pool. I ordered a beer enjoyed a cigarette, because oddly enough you could smoke in this health spa.

I was to meet up with two other guys for this conference, Jos from the Netherlands and a new guy to our little turf travels group called Russel. They had sent me a message and said that they had checked into the hotel and asked if I would like to join them.

I said that I was already in the bar by the pool, and knowing that they would also have to go through the same corridor of death that I had, I was amused by not telling them in advance. I ordered the beer for them and waited.

Five mins went by, and they both call asking as to where I was.

"By the pool", I said, and gave them directions.

They then realised that they were in different hotels.

We had pre-planned to stay in the same hotel as the conference. The Radisson we all agreed. But there were three different Radisson hotels here in the retreat, and we had managed to book a room in all three. Since I had already ordered the beer, the other two finally found me. We compared the corridors of death as each of us had our own in our individual hotels. We have photos, and they just make it look worse.

We compare the room facilities in the hotels we had booked. It worked out that the Jos had the best with an included mini-bar and large balcony and the hotel boasted two bars and restaurants overlooking the pool. I had the mid-range one that at least had a bar and restaurant with my room having a coffee machine. Russel had obviously booked last, and his hotel had nothing. Not even a front desk. He had to use one of either of ours. With the piss-take carrying on for some time on that topic we decided on the restaurant for dinner.

The following morning we met in the breakfast room at my hotel, still taking the piss that Russel had to walk through his corridor of death before getting to the outside world. The breakfast was delicious, and soon enough, we joined with other delegates and head for the busses outside to take us to the university where we were to spend the day educating ourselves.

The presentations were a mixed bag, as always it is with these things. I know and have probably presented both enthusiastically and dull. There was one guy that sounded like a robot and another who could have come straight out of a Japanese cartoon. But I should not criticise as presenting is a skill you learn over time.

After a standing networking meal, we headed on the busses to a fascinating place that trials grasses in all sorts of situations. They even assist in the development of chemicals and bio-stimulant products—an engaging and professional site.

About 6 pm we walk to a converted house and barn for our dinner in the rain. It started with small plates of delightful Italian cheeses and ham, and at that time we thought that was it, especially since it was all coming out of the back of a transit van. So we filled ourselves as much as possible. When the main course arrived we could not face any more food.

Back to the hotel Jos, Russel and I decided a nightcap would be a good idea. So we went to the best hotel of the three for an excellent local wine. Whilst out having a smoke, I heard the sound of music coming from my hotel.

Being weak and having a massive fear of missing out, I go back in and tell the others to finish their drinks so we can head over to my hotel and see what the noise was all about. It certainly was better than the quiet and rather empty bar that we were in.

Gatecrashing the party of well-known chemical manufacture in our industry is always good fun, We helped ourselves to a beer and joined in with the staff members.

Morning came, and we compared our terrible nights of sleep. The rain had arrived, and it was grey and English looking outside. We set off towards a very nice golf course where the event would carry on inside their member's room for presentations to be followed by a course walk. I choose this time to have meetings with my Italian and Portuguese distributor as it made sense to save further trips, and I was not so interested in listening to competitors going through their product presentations.

Apart from putting my foot in it with forgetting how one of the Italian federation board members looked like, and asking if he worked on the course, all was well. Networking was excellent, and I met many Greenkeepers and researchers in the turf industry. Over another standing lunch of a selection of more Italian meats, I decide that I would skip the course walk and answer some emails and complete a little work that was backing up. I sat on the front verandah of the clubhouse in the sun and opened up the iPad.

The next bus trip was to a botanical garden in Padua. It is such a beautiful city. Since I had been to the garden before, I decided to go for a local cultural walk while the others looked at plants. Jos and Russel joined me together with a German professor. We walked around the city, bought a few packs of cigarettes and then sat down in a cafe and had a drink and people watched. The main square had a circus of sorts and dodgems. I suggested it, but nobody wanted to join me. Back to work, we headed back into the bus, which was now getting lighter as people dropped off—no idea where they went, but they were undoubtedly disappearing.

The last destination was the local rugby teams training ground and a red machinery demonstration. Followed by a bbq and finish to the conference.

Getting back to our collection of hotels was quick for a change. We thanked our mad Italian bus driver and hit the bar with the remainder of the delegation.

Unusual to find within the turf industry such musical talent. One of the machine sales guys was on the piano and singing. He was brilliant and a joy to listen to and to finish these two days with some live music was perfect.

Soon after, one of the more prominent delegates' wife stepped in and played. Wow. Between them both they had everyone singing and clapping along—such enjoyment.

During the singing and under the influence of wine, I may have suggested that I would drop off some guys at the airport on my way to meet with my Italian distributor. Which to their surprise in the morning was to be in my little fiat 500 hire car. This was actually not that bad—four medium-sized blokes with carry-on luggage in a micro Italian vehicle.

Leaving them at the airport, I went on my way south to meet my distributor and a customer close to San Marino. Having never visited there, I was looking very much forward to the evening walk up to the top and enjoy the views.

But first, there was a 3-hour drive to overcome. I had planned it so I would be able to have one hour lunchtime side stop at Imola. Being a Formula 1 freak, I had always wanted to visit the track and more specifically, the park that sits within it. It hosts the monument to Senna. Parking up at the main paddock I popped into the info section and bought a senna cap for my collection of travel bits. I knew it was only a ten mins walk under the track and then into the park. You get excellent views of the track and also the spot where the fateful crash happened. It is covered in flags and notes from fans. The monument is very nice. Although a few Mercedes AMG cars were going around, the place was peaceful. A beautiful place to reflect on a fantastic legend.

Off to meet at the golf course next. And having gone through a few products that may suit their program we headed off to San Marino.

San Marino. Or I should say the Most Serene Republic of San Marino. It is only about 60km2 and a population of about 30,000 inhabitants. Being one of the wealthiest countries in the world by GDP and has more cars than people. Its location high on a hill has always interested me. The views I have seen are spectacular, and with a 360degree view of Italy from its castle top, It is a must if you are in the region.

Following a bus, up the winding roads, I could not fully enjoy the drive. At one point the bus had to do a three-point turn to get around one of the hairpins. We enter the clouds, and that was the end of my view. I parked in a lift at the hotel and then went for a walk in the dimness. The visibility was 20 m, so I just wandered around in moisture.

Still, there were many tourists, mostly of Asian origin. I looked at a tourist shop and was very close to buying a waving dancing trump ornament but since the family has decided not to purchase unnecessary plastics I did not. Still, the options were Trump, the Pope and Mr Bean. And to do them justice on my shelf of shit I had to buy all three. So I walked off empty-handed.

I then discover a little further down the hill towards the hotel that half the shops were selling guns and massive knives. Weird. But then I found a toy car shop, so I went in and bought a Landrover—an excellent memory of this apparently breathtaking place.

My hotel was Grand San Marino, and I have to say that sounds up there, but it is not. The room overlooks a rock face, and there was no working WiFi or mobile network. Everything was a little tired. Which is probably why the carpet towards my room is covered in plastic and a man was painting. But inside my room were two large white fluffy towels. Perfect.

On returning to the hotel and freshening up I caught up with the family. Being late evening now I headed out in search of a restaurant. The whole place was dead. But the clouds were starting to give way to some spectacular mini views. I could see the coast at one point, but the clouds came back, and it disappeared.

Having found nothing that looked interesting, I went back to the hotel and was in for a surprise. The restaurant was offering a five-course tasting menu of local dishes. Perfect and for €22 you can't go wrong with that. I am not a food critic but this was a properly lovely meal which would certainly do well on Masterchef.

Many things have woken me up in hotel rooms in the past, but the sanding of walls just outside my room is a first. I open my door to scaffolding. Again a first. A man popped his head down from it. I almost shouted but did not. I spoke in a sarcastic and irritated way the I was not impressed with this at 7:30 am. I got dressed and went to check out and have breakfast before asking a man to bring my car down from the top of the lift.

A four-hour drive back to Venice I looked forward to getting home to what was left of my children's half term. However, with a few weeks break from travel to make up a bit at home, the next trip is to be Prague, no doubt my favourite city in Europe.

15. Czech Rep June 2019

With only two days before my family and I move from our house in the UK and off to Sweden, I managed to book this little trip. Naturally, it did not go down well with Lina as she was left with the last days of cleaning the rental house in the UK and with all the final bits of organising left to do that weekend it was undoubtedly a little stressful.

Still, I needed to visit my customers in Prague before the summer holidays and my move, and with limited time in the diary for the rest of year work had to come first.

Visiting my three customers at their three different golf courses and then meeting up for dinner and a few beers nothing exciting happened. There was banter and there was industry chat. A standard trip really, building the relationships with the guys.

If I am honest when it came to writing this chapter I found that I had not made any notes from the trip. And I could not remember the details. I was going to ignore this trip but then that felt like I was ignoring the trip in total so I thought that I would write a little about Prague itself, as it is my favourite city on the continent.

Prague or Praha is the historic capital of Bohemia and has been the residence of several Roman Emperors, most well known is Charles IV. Looking over the city is Prague Castle, built in the 9th century. Well worth the clime up the stairs to visit. More dominant is the cathedral, which began its build in 1344 but was not fully completed until well in the 20th century. It is protected by so many wonderful gargoyles that are quite simply scary.

Another iconic construction is the Charles Bridge. It has been used as the backdrop of so many films. Built under the watchful eye of the Holy Roman Emperor Charles IV having placed the foundation stone at 5:31am on the 9th of July 1357. I don't think I have ever been to the city without walking across it. I recall once the mist was so dense that the other side was invisible. Walking into nothing but dimly visible lights and listening the roaring water below is something I will never forget.

During the Second World War Hitler took over the Castle and most of the Jews were killed or deported away. The Jewish cemetery is situated on the new side of the city close the Charles bridge and I recommend anyone to visit to get a feel for the atrocities that happened during the Nazi occupation of the city.

As a young boy I don't know why but I was fascinated by Czechoslovakia and found the flag to be my favourite of all the flags of the world. I longed to visit. I never did. When the Velvet Revolution took place in 1989 I remember watching on the news. In 1993 Prague became the capital of the new Czech Republic and has prospered ever since.

I first visited the city in the early 2000s and was so in awe of the city I longed to revisit each time I left. Having been there many times now I still feel a sense of history here, I cant quite put my finger on it but if you brush the strip bars, the drunk stags, and the tourist groups aside ,and look at the city for what it is you will see that it has gone through so much and it still looks beautiful, really beautiful.

I know I have not done the city justice in writing this. Go and feel it yourself, you will not be disappointed.

Back to the UK for what to be my final week before moving to Sweden. A new home, a new house and a new hub to fly from.

16. UK July 2019

As I have mentioned previously, returning to Sweden after many years as ex-pats, both in the UK and Africa, it is strange to fly to the UK for a meeting and then leave. My role as European Sales Manger with the company I work for had started in January 2019 being the influence for this book. Now it takes on a new chapter, literally.

Travelling around Europe from the UK is very easy. Both London Heathrow and Gatwick are good hubs to get around with minimal stopovers and changes. Luxury in the travelling world. My new base is to be Stockholm. Stockholm is not a lousy hub either, but we had purchased a house 2 hours away from the airport by car, and 3 hours by airport transfer coach. This meant that that my total travel time would increase a bit.

We had moved the on the last week of June with the moving in date being the 1st of July. This was all exciting and the family could not be happier living in our own home for the first time in almost ten years of renting. However, we had a company sales and marketing meeting that I needed to attend on the 3rd. This meant that I needed to leave Sweden on the 2nd to be on time for the meeting. So, after being in my new house for less than 24 hours, I am on the road again.

Thankfully I persuaded Lina to drive me to the bus station so I could catch my bus to the airport. With no coffee before we left, I was looking forward to enjoying a cup on the bus. I had booked a first-class seat for about £3 more, and it showed on the website that I would be able to have breakfast included. This was not the case, but the seat on the bus was very comfortable, and I slept for a good while. Note to self that if this is a way of travel then must bring own coffee. I must invest in one of those collapsible cup things.

On the plane, I am positioned next to a family with two young boys. One which moaned all the way. The other played sonic the fucking blue hedgehog, collecting coins, or whatever, at high volume. Not even my noise-cancelling headphones could deal with this. The father was sitting next to me, looking at very odd pictures of cats, signs, and cakes. Not being sure if it had something to do with his work I could not help myself from looking at the pictures too. He took time to take in each photo. Still baffled, I tried to distract myself with my book.

I am picked up at Heathrow by my colleague Bradley who informed me that I am to be dropped directly off at the pub. Having no issue with this at all, we caught up chatting on the way. Now I should say that we always meet in a pub in the very English village of Yattendon. I always look forward to staying in this place. The food is brilliant and the atmosphere very relaxed.

The Royal Oak has about ten rooms, and throughout the years, I think I have stayed in every room. Each named after a gun manufacturer. I was to be in Winchester for the two nights. A good room, I must say, and probably my favourite.

I unpack my bag, have a quick shower in the complicated bath set up. I find that it is always challenging to get the temperature right in the two tap system. Anyway, the sun was shining, the temperature outside perfect. I took the iPad outside with a tasty British Ale to keep me company I prepared my work for the meeting.

The beer garden started to fill up, and there were a few girls, probably in their early 20's, discussing their issues with their morning horse ride. Either it was too hot, or the animal was too small and needed replacing with a larger one. It was quite intriguing to listen to serious first world problems. One of the girls took this opportunity with her friends to voice her new plan to make lots of money. The plan it turned out was the acquiring of two dogs and then breeding them. Sounded like a straightforward and effortless way to cover the cost of her handbag.

I changed my attention to the Lionesses on the television. It was an epic game, but unfortunately, they got knocked out. I ordered some dinner and shortly afterwards headed for a good nights sleep.

I am picked up early by Sharon, another colleague, and we head for our office and spent the day covering the whole company world wide business. It was good to see everyone. It is strange having to be taxied around due to my Land Rover being still out of action and in storage in Chichester. After the days work, we all head back to *The Royal Oak* for a company dinner with a few wines. I was looking forward to flying home though and spending some time in our new family home with a few weeks vacation away from travel.

The first trip after the summer break was to be Lithuania. The first visit to a club that is so far out there in its design that I still can't quite visualise that it is real.

17. Lithuania August 2019

Being the first real trip from my new home, it felt odd—a new way to go to the airport. A new car to go in too. My Land Rover being still in the UK storage we had leased a Golf. A very red and fast car. We like it. And to be honest, you can't go wrong with the VW Golf. It is bulletproof, comfortable and bigger inside than you might think.

Just in time, I worked out the slightly confusing way to pay for parking in the long stay car park and jumped on my train to Stockholm. I do like Swedish trains. They are quieter and cleaner than that of most trains I travel on. There is always space to sit also. A little sleep later and we arrive at Stockholm central station. I swapped trains to the fast one to Arlanda Airport and went in search of the new American Express lounge where I have read you can order a full breakfast at no cost for just having a credit card.

It turns out you can't. Or I did not have the right card. Anyway, I enjoyed the cheese sandwich, and a couple of coffees then went for a walk to find the smoking cabin.

My flight to Copenhagen went quickly with nothing to speak of really. I had a short connection time to catch my flight to Vilnius. Getting to my gate, I see the micro-plane that is to take me on the two-hour flight. I had flown further away on an A320neo brand new jet to turn around and get on a twin-prop. I always feel uneasy on prop aircraft.

Boarding, I discover the plane is full with a Lithuanian national team. No idea what sport they play but whatever sport it is there is about 16 of them plus two management or coach people.

The Airport in Vilnius is unusual. It is not modern by any means, and small. I like it. Easy to get around. The total time it took to get from the plane to the Uber that I ordered whilst walking from the plane was 8 minutes. This is, to me, travel in its most perfect form.

On researching a little about Lithuania before my visit, I discovered that it was once a considerable part of Europe covering from the Baltic coast to Ukraine. Furthermore, it was the first Baltic State to declare independence from the former Soviet Union in 1990. I had not been to the country before and was interested to see if there was much difference with its neighbour Latvia. Unfortunately, I was not to spend any time at all in the capital. I was only over for one night, and that was to be at the complex of the golf course.

The golf course I am visiting is only twenty minutes away in a hideous Skoda Roomster Uber car. And arriving at the hotel, I was greeted by my host, and we caught up over a coffee.

The hotel looked huge. And I mean it stretched out over a vast area. Only the spa section of the Vilnius Grand Hotel, that was not yet open at the time of writing, stands probably the same size as most big hotels. My room was very nice, fluffy white towels included and a good size bed.

After a quick refresh, I went down to meet up with the course manager. We met in the main lobby bar overlooking the lake. I noticed an odd, slightly out of place waterside bar and restaurant. I am told that it is a Thai style beach bar. We immediately walked towards it to see if it was open and offering some dinner.

Sitting in the Thai Beach bar aptly named the Bora Bora, we enjoy dinner washed down with the few local brews. The evening goes on, and we discuss his new plans for the course along with filling me in on how it is like to live in Lithuania.

The restaurant is quiet, only two other tables are filled. One group was a Russian woman with her two children and what initially looked like her mother. This turned out to be the nanny. The nanny took care of the children whilst the mother stood in the evening sun, taking selfies of herself. Although she was beautiful, it seemed a far cry from our usual way of life.

After a late breakfast the following day we go for a drive around the golf course. It is undoubtedly one the very few courses that I have been too that has that much water on it—a very well maintained course. With lunchtime looming and my flight back coming closer to reality, we finalised the business side to the trip, and then I grab an Uber to the airport. On the short drive back to the city I was trying to soak the atmosphere in for the country. I must come back to accomplish that fully. Lithuania warrants a closer inspection.

In the airport, I picked up two small novelty shot glasses in the most terrible packaging for my cupboard of shit. At least I managed that.

Another new place next week. Iceland. A country I have looked forward to visiting for a very long time.

18. Iceland August 2019

Since we had moved to Sweden, we borrowed a Land Rover from friends in Stockholm. They were on vacation with their other Land Rover in Croatia, so they had offered us to use their 110 Defender until they were to return and we had a chance to either sort out ours or get hold of another vehicle. It had been a help as we were able to use its vast space for furniture transport and general moving of stuff while we were getting settled. Since we had now received the Golf we had arranged that on this trip I would drive to Stockholm to drop the Land Rover off and spend the night with them before my Icelandic trip.

As it is when you catch up with old friends, it becomes a late night, but with a 4 am start this is never smart. So in the taxi, I slept my way to the airport for my first of two flights to Reykjavík.

I discovered the WiFi onboard, and I found out that I had to pick my hire car up and then head towards a golf course just north of Reykjavik that Einar managed, he would be my guide for all things turf in Iceland.

On arrival, we had a coffee, and then I was informed of the itinerary for the two-day visit. It would consist of quite a bit of driving and quite a bit of wind. Still, I was excited to see as much as possible of the country. The place is just magical to look at, and I had hoped to see a few of the sights. In fact, I knew we were going to visit the blue lagoon, so I was looking forward to bathing in the superheated natural turquoise water that is used in so many marketing pictures of Iceland.

First, we visited one grass football pitch, which is uncommon apparently in Iceland, and then we headed off to a golf course on the coastline a bit south of the capital.

If you can imagine a links-style golf course but remove the gorse and heather and replace it with black volcanic rock, you are close to the unreal and raw landscape that is this golf course. Simply amazing. Now I take photos of most of the venues I go to, mostly these are signature holes famed for their design and beauty and used to market the venue. But here I could not stop taking landscape pictures of almost every hole we drove down.

We discussed the weather, naturally, and I found out that there is not so much snow but rain and wind. In the summer it is around 15 degrees and windy with the winter being much colder and even more wind. The weather can change so fast here. There is even an app that you download to let you know when the road is closed.

I forgot to mention the hire car as I usually do. The hire car was dismal, a Kia of sorts. I don't know what. But it was warm and protected me from the wind, so I liked it very much.

At about 5 pm we parted company, and I went to the hotel. Had a sulphur shower and changed for dinner. I was to meet up again with Einar, and he had asked me what I would like. I suggested that we go local. I want to try the local dishes whenever I am in a new place, and puffin, whale, and smoked lamb was on the menu at one place, so we went for that.

What was it like? Amazing! But seven small tasting courses did fill us up. Mostly the food tasted either smokey or fishy, with puffin and blend of both. Washed down with some of the worlds most expensive beer we finished and decided to call it a day. In compensation, I lifted the tweezers that I ate my puffin with to put into my cupboard of shit.

I slept like a baby. I awoke early with the time difference of two hours, which I have to be honest I forgot about. I headed back to the course where I was to make my presentation and introduce both myself and the company I work for to the Icelandic Greenkeepers and Groundsman. I always get nervous about doing this. But it is the easiest way to meet a bunch of new people. I had prepared well, and it was merely an introduction and not technical in any way.

After the presentation, I was invited with my guide for lunch at the nearest golf club to the club we were at. This was another opportunity to see some more fantastic scenery and see how they dealt with the enormous amount of play and lack of time to do any serious maintenance work. With so much light in the summer months, the amount of golf is unreal compared to many places.

There is a fantastic fact about golf in Iceland. The population of Iceland is roughly 330,000 people. It has more than 60 golf courses!

The last golf course of my visit was to be one I will never forget. Of all the courses that I have been to in both my work and private life, all over the world, I have never taken photos of every single hole. As I mentioned earlier, it is just bite-the-back-of-your-hand gorgeous. I did not even notice the cold sideways blasting wind.

With the evening spent walking around the city and finding somewhere to eat that would not have the expense account bursting at the seams. I found a cosy little bar and restaurant and spent the time people watching over a simple local lamb dish. I wished to maximise my time here, so I got up at 4 am the following morning and went for the 2-hour drive to the geyser collection, and oh my god it was worth it. I spent 20 mins there as I had to head for the airport to catch my plane.

The road back was just out of this world—volcanic fields with a clear sky. I took far too many photos from the empty highway than was possibly legal. I spoke aloud in the car at the spectacular views and reflected on this first visit to Iceland.

I did not mention cars. Sorry, the Icelandic 4x4s. These things are big. They make my Land Rover Defender look small and pointless. 38inch wheels and diff guards like walls. I even saw one Landcruiser with the capability to spray water from little outlets on its tyres. A proper volcano exploration vehicle. And being a Landrover person I did see some equally cool arctic setups that I guess would be utterly useless in most of Europe, but I would still like to have one.

Housing is minimalistic in Iceland. The houses are low but so Scandinavian in their design. Very cool and open, allowing the light to get to every corner of either the house or apartment.

My flight to Oslo from Reykjavík was a smooth one and landing in Oslo I swiftly went to the notice board to check the flight to Stockholm. The flight was showing that was to be delayed by ten mins. Now I always get a little worried if a flight is delayed by only a short while, it is better to be honest and inform you that your fucked for an hour. You can make arrangements and go and sit down and have a drink or something. So after the third 10 minute delay, I left the standing line and went for a beer.

This delay had messed up my train home, so I need to stay overnight at friends in Stockholm which was acceptable but not ideal. I do like to get home after being away. There is nothing better than your own bed. Still, I had the most enjoyable Friday evening in Stockholm under the influence with friends.

Next week I shall up the temperature a little by visiting Slovenia via Zurich.

19. Slovenia August 2019

Two 0'clock in the morning is no time to get up, for any reason. It is the time that most people are in deep eye fluttering sleep. Thinking that the only thing that could make the strain of getting out of bed worse was to have my duvet filled with wasps, the taxi picking me up called to say that he was lost. Again, this is made further complicated with the fact that his Swedish was more broken than mine, and he spoke only a little English, so directions were strained and quite vague.

Finally, we met along the roadside a short walk from my house we rushed towards the bus station in Örebro. Inside the airport, I went to the lounge for some breakfast. This time it was the old SAS business lounge, and it was very disappointing, just bread, cheese and smoked ham. Not perfect, but the coffee was good. Thankfully I get this perk for free. I would have been very disappointed to pay the full price of entrance.

Taxiing out of the terminal the plane to Zurich, my, we encountered a technical issue, my first for many years. The stewardess informs us that we have to pull over to the side and have the mechanics look at the problem. So it seems that the plane could not get its GPS to work. This is important, I guess. We need to know where we are going or where we are. Finally, we are given the go-ahead to depart.

It is always challenging to ask two people to move out of their seat so you can go to the toilet on a short flight. I mean, why did you not go before you get onboard? Well, I could not hold it any longer. The pregnant woman and her husband moved out struggling a little.

On arriving at Zurich, the transit desk was my aim. Knowing already that I had missed my connection flight to Ljubljana, I am informed that it would be later in the day. Well, early evening in fact. So I would have to lose quite a bit of my trip. The next available flight out was 8:45 pm and that I had to wait around for 9 hours. Thankfully the transit guy told me to get my new boarding pass from the first transit desk I went to, only ten mins walk away. I went there to be told no! I must go back to get it at the desk I had just come from. Since I had time, this was something to do. I had no urgency. Just the desire to sit down in one of the most decorative and smoker-friendly lounges I have ever seen at an airport.

Once I finally got my pass, I slipped into the smoking lounge. Then onward to the other airport lounge to catch up with some work. It makes no difference to me where I am as long as I have some internet, a seat, and sometimes a power socket. This spot was perfect.

I am writing now from within the lounge. I have been here for 7 hours now. And I have something to report. The lounge has been vacated, and now there are only eight others left in here. A large section of the room has been cornered off for some VIP guests. I guess the difference to me and you are that the VIP guests don't have to walk the three meters it is to the bar for drinks as a selection has been set out in small buckets of ice. Protected by rope, we wait with bated breath who is so important that they require this.

Sorry to disappoint you but I left before the Vip's arrived and I was not going to stay one minute longer. Meeting my distributor after an uneventful flight over the alps at night, we head directly for my hotel and have a quick catch up over a beer. Two beers later, I had been awake for 22 hours and now starting to flail. The bed was needed.

I woke up about 3 seconds before my alarm and panicked I had overslept. I hit the snooze button and finally came too at 6:45 am. I packed up my stuff and went down for some coffee. I was surprised to find the breakfast room filled with elderly Germans, all lining up, or not lining up as it happens, for the various selection of food offerings. One older woman directly barged passed me and grabbed the roll I had my eye on. Anyway, I had my mind focused on what would be a very long day—meeting some old clients of my distributor but also some new potential customers too. We visited three big football venues, including the national stadium as well as a most picturesque golf course. At the golf course, we discussed the future plans of our company with our distributor and the Slovenian Greenkeepers Association, both of which guys were on the board.

At one point during a football club visitation, we bumped into a sales rep for another company. Now I get on with most of our competitors, and I even have a few beers with them at events we all end up at. And as I have mentioned, we go even as far as booking the same hotels so we can have some company at after the working day is done. Here it is different. It is not that they can't speak or shake hands; they do that; it is the backtalk—anyway sales politics. I am not going into that. I trust everyone once.

So back in the truck, we headed to drop me at the airport, but on the way, lunch is discussed. And so in agreement that it would be a great idea, we diverted to an Italian restaurant and sat outside in the warming sun and ate delicious pasta whilst analysing and digesting the visits we had made.

Now I have written about Ljubljana airport before. It gives the impression of stepping back in time. Now I can report that since my last visit there have been some significant changes. There is construction going on at the time of writing to develop a large new international terminal. Suppose you don't travel like me then you probably don't care. But now you know anyway.

I checked the bag in and found myself given the priority pass to go through even though I was not flying in any priority level nor have I yet reached the level required with "Star Alliance" to have it. But you don't kick these moments of opportunity away. So I walked to the front of the long queue of people. I hear comments as I walk down, and then I am asked twice to look at my boarding card. I must look non deserved of this privilege. But with a wave of arrogance only gained by this free opportunity, I walked through and went directly to buy some duty-free cigarettes.

On the bus to the plane, we are stopped by a military guard lineup. A Hungarian dignitary had obviously either arrived or was leaving in their military private jet parked close to the terminal. It was quite a sight to see, and relatively pointless to have the guard lineup, but there you go. I did not see any media or press, so not sure who was benefiting.

After a very smooth flight over to Zurich, I went in search of the giant board to show me where the gate was for my flight to Stockholm. I was in horror to see it was red. Oh No! not another delay. And it was ten mins too. Nothing is ever ten minutes late.

I walked around the airport a little as I could not sit down any more, and looked in the many shops Zurich airport has to offer. Surprisingly enough, you can buy Swiss Army knives. I thought it would be fun to do so. But then I have a few so it would be pointless.

Now I like to think of myself as an avid and well-travelled person. I do not stress in airports. I quite like the buzz. But I made a stupid error in reading the gate number for my Stockholm bound flight. I was heading toward passport control. Odd, I thought, but then I am in Switzerland, and maybe I need it. But I should not need one on this trip, even though I have both of mine with me. So I asked the question to the passport officer.

"Am I in the right place for the flight to Stockholm?"

"No!" she said.

She promptly pointed me in the direction of the secret way out of the passport section. I guessed that it must be used for those with fake documents and the stupid who cant read departure boards.

Arriving at the correct gate, I make it just in time for my exactly ten minutes delayed flight. I sit back, relax, and listen to an audio-book for a while for I have one more plane to get into this evening. Well, to stay in actually. I had looked at all the airport hotels in Stockholm and found that they were too overpriced for what I wanted. I needed a bed, just a bed, nothing more, and it needed to be close to the terminal for my early morning flight to Vienna.

So I had booked the Jumbo Hotel. Yes, it is an old 747 that has been converted into a hostel/hotel. My room was to be one of the four engines. No ensuite but hey, I am going to sleep in an engine of a 747, and that is all that matters.

I shall revert in the next chapter on how it was. Tomorrow, back across Europe to Vienna, what a week.

20. Austria September 2019

So firstly I must report on the previous nights stay in the engine of a jumbo jet. The check-in was simple enough, climb the stairs to the main entrance of the beast and then take your shoes off! I forgot this is Sweden. The only country in the world where you take your shoes off to enter a mechanics workshop. After checking in at the reception and bar in the old first-class nose section of the aircraft I put my boots back on and walked back down the stairs in the wind and rain towards the right-hand side furthest engine.

The room itself was wobbly. There was enough room for a double bed, and that was about it. The toilet was obviously in the central part of the plane. As well as the communal shower. I threw my bags into the engine and then went back to the first-class section in the nose of the aircraft for a drink. It was late, and I needed a wind-down. With a beer in hand, I walked over to the wing exit and walked down the wing. It was quite cool. Not often you get this chance to do this.

I slept very well in the engine. It was a little noisy if I am honest, but it worked. I had to get up for the 6:30 am plane to Vienna, so it did not matter that much. At 4 am I forced a coffee and sandwich down and headed for the bus transfer to the terminal. I had plans of sleeping on this flight or at least trying to.

I have just looked back to see if I could capture the attention of a flight steward to get some coffee and my eyes can't believe what I can see. Open-mouthed sleeping people. Lots of them. A horrific sight. This brings to mind *The Hitchhikers Guide to the Galaxy* where there was a slight delay on a ship in some galactic spaceport, the passengers were all put in "suspended animation" due to a "slight delay" whilst waiting for lemon soaked napkins to be loaded onto the ship. When they are woken once a year for coffee and biscuits they scream. After thousands of years you can't blame them.

The hotel I had chosen to stay on this trip I had been to before. I did not hold much hope for room to ready any minute earlier than the stated 3 pm check in time. I was right. I mean, there is no way that there is no room ready. That would mean that the cleaners had done nothing until midday. Since I had had one visit to a golf course and one had cancelled, I was early to the hotel. Quite common in our business and we accept that greenkeepers and groundsmen have so much to do in such a tight time frame. Seeing a salesman is the first thing to be knocked off of the schedule. I had a coffee while waiting for my room right in front of the receptionist so that it would keep her reminded that I was very irritated and desired my room the moment the cleaners had finished with whatever they were not doing.

That evening I went down to my Austrian local for a beer and dinner. Nice to have these spots. Where you walk in after a few months away and you still are greeted by name. The chef came out and sorted me the mother of fish and chips. Feeling at the bursting point, I headed back to my hotel for an evening of "Poldark" on TV and sleep.

Breakfast was busy. A room filled with busloads of Asian tourists. All with their face masks and two backpacks each. Funny how they have breakfast. I grabbed mine and headed out for my calls—long drives out of Vienna. On the way, another call for which was booked later in the afternoon cancelled on me too. We made another arrangement, and I filled my day seeing someone else not on my original list.

I sort of know my way around these golf courses now but still partly rely on the GPS to get closer. I made a wrong turning leaving one club and ended up on a cycle path. After the third Austrian on a bike stopped me and pointing out I was "wrong road" I joined a roundabout via the path and left the area quickly. From someone who has driven from Sweden to Africa on a year overland trip using the most basic of GPS mapping software I am very embarrassed at admitting this. At least I have not put a foot in a Venetian canal whilst drunk and hunting for my hotel so it could be worse.

Anyway, back at the hotel, I planned to shower, change, and negotiate the tram to the central part of the city. I knew you could buy the tickets on the tram itself as I had found out by roughly working it out with my rubbish German knowledge. What I did not anticipate was the volume of the machine. Everything I was doing was shouted out to everyone on board. As I had pressed the English button, it was a case of spot the tourist.

So another Irish bar for dinner in Vienna. I must change this. The problem is that I only go where the greenkeepers drink. This city breaks my rules for going local. I was to meet with a few guys to chat over a pint.

While waiting, I Googled some bars in Vienna and found a great site that showed a list of quirky bars. Right up my street. I found the closest—*Loos bar*. The decor is like being brought back to the 1920s in the USA. The place is fantastic if you like cocktails, which I don't. Very small but very quaint. I order a Vespa.. just because it reminded me of a bond movie. But dressed in jeans and a fleece, it was odd. The drink, on the other hand, was far to easy to drink. So now to the lavatory. Well, the bar is small, and the facilities are through a short steep staircase below. I clime down slowly admiring the pictures of 1920's culture on the wall. Would you believe it, there, at the bottom, is a woman just sitting down next to a small table. She is the cleaner and requires tips. This is so American. And on the basis I had no cash, she did not get a tip. If I am honest I don't really know the order of things when it comes to lavatory attendants. I don't even know what their proper name is. The lady had a huge array of perfumes, cigarettes, creams and cufflinks. I just don't get why. She is basically in a hole in a small bar and hoping that a guy, desperate for a pee after his third martini needs to then purchase cufflinks and a new smell. If I was a woman and a guy returned from the lavatory with a new overpowering fragrance I would think that something had not gone well and needs covering up. In fact, I do not need to write "if I was a woman" there. I would think that anyway.

I was to fly Austrian Airlines on this Friday travel day home, and it is nice to note that the airline still offers free drinks and a snack onboard their planes. This is rare now in the European airspace. But then again the cost of the flight is usually slightly more.

So as I type now I am enjoying the inflight drinks trolly. Thank You Austrian! It has been a long week. Just a 3-hour bus ride left.

Next week I shall be travelling to the UK for a week both for a marketing meeting in the head office and then some time staying back in the last village I used to live. It will be great to catch up with old mates and back to Goodwood for the Revival Meeting.

21. UK September 2019

Another 2 am morning waking up with the stressful feeling of hope that the taxi driver finds the house in time. Sleeping on the bus is uncomfortable and I cant settle down. It is difficult even if you have a travel pillow and unique fleece that covers your face with its hood, noise-cancelling headphones and an eye mask. The problem is the angle of the seat. And I guess this is true for any seat when you are so tired that you ache.

Arriving at Arlanda Airport, I meet with a colleague in the security line. We meet another on the other side for breakfast. We had a quick catch up and then headed off in search of Swedish chocolate to buy for the guys in the office as a gift. Swedish chocolate is underrated within the chocolate world. It is very good indeed, and the office knows it. Therefore I try to always bring some over for them.

Depending on where you sit on a plane, you have the luck as to when you will be served. Now I like to be as near to the front as possible but always just behind the wing. I understand that this is one of the most comfortable sections of the plane as it is effected the least during turbulence. Unfortunately, this part of the aircraft can be either the first or the last place to have the drinks trolley arrive. On the day I need coffee, and willing to pay for it, I am the last to be served. Unhappy face.

In London, we are met by our marketing manager Bradley, and

are taken directly to our head office for the marketing meeting. The marketing and product meeting went well, with lots of new stuff to go out in the new year and for us to inform our customers.

As always we are to finish the day in the *Royal Oak* pub in Yattendon. I have mentioned this place before. We all like it. And we all want to stay there too. We were to enjoy an evening of a hog roast with many wines. And the food does not disappoint.

As I was to be in the UK for the rest of the week, I spent the day in the office catching up with things like expenses. The other guys all left. Mid-afternoon I am given a lift to the train station for my trip to Bosham.

The evening is spent with some friends in the pub, my old local, and it was nice to catch up with them. My new office for the rest of the week was to be the kitchen table at my brothers house. I had made arrangements to meet up with my old cycle partner, and we hit our old path up the South Downs. It was a great ride, naturally followed by a pint and pork scratching or two to balance out the calories. It is nice to look forward to getting outside for something during the day. I am not sure I could have an office-based job where I would be stuck inside for most of the day. I do feel fortunate doing what I do and having the freedom in which to do so.

Now my brother Dominic can't cook, and, when I got back from the ride, I needed a shower as I was to meet up with other friends at the pub later that evening. As I went off for a shower, I shouted to him to finely cut up an onion and some celery. He called back that he had not cut an onion before. Not believing him, I ignored him. Fresh and changed I went to the kitchen and finished chopping the hacked onion and made dinner. He does rely on his partner for food, Thankfully I was there, or he probably would not have eaten.

Friday, being The Revival Golf day at Goodwood with an early start I am dressed in tweed and plus-fours waiting for my friend Rob to drive us to the club. Being the Revival weekend, the roads around

Goodwood are filled with the smell of real petrol and millions of pounds of classic cars.

It also meant that we were late for the shotgun start. With one bag of hickory clubs to share the golf was quite ok and once we got used to which "machie" we were to use on each type of shot we got the hang of it. I lost almost all of Robs' golf balls. But since he had hit himself twice within two visits to a bunker, it was equal of piss-take for the day.

Back at the clubhouse, we waited for our name not to be called out for the prize giving. Failing to win anything we headed for the track. The way to the track is simple from the golf course. You stand outside by the road in a line and wait for the vintage cars to take you down to the race track, we got an old series 2a Land Rover, so I was the happiest person there.

The Revival is a must-see event at Goodwood. It is where one of the most expensive race grid in the world is held. The "Kinrara" trophy. A blend of Mustang's, Jaguar's, Aston Martins, Porsche's, and Ferrari's to name but a few race in the sunset of the Goodwood motor circuit. I love it and have to agree with myself that I will attend every year.

But that race was later. The afternoon was also a time to see and hear beautiful specimens from days gone by either racing or doing demonstration drives. It is also a place where you get the chance to see some fantastic flying machines. Rob and I waited in line to go in a DC3, something I had not done before and him being a pilot he got to sit in his captain's seat. Another friend called Richard phoned to see where were and it happened to be great timing as he could take the paparazzi shots of us in the cockpit from outside. We wandered around looking at Spitfires and other planes I don't know.

Time for the race, and what a race it is. The glorious sun setting in the background. There is nothing more that I can write that give justice to this perfect setting for an evening in September. You need to go there. End.

Back at my brothers, Rob and I have a wonderful curry waiting for us cooked by Dominic's partner Suki. What a great extra few days catching up with old friends, with the chance to experience the Goodwood Revival too.

Saturday was to be a long travel day. Getting home finally at 9 pm I embraced the whole family. With only one day at home before a week of work in Norway, it is all too brief.

22. Norway September 2019

Being the third pre 3 am start in a row the novelty, I must say, is beginning to wear a little thin. I need to sort my Land Rover out or get another car here just for airport trips. The idea of leaving the day before and staying in a cheap airport hotel is also starting to appeal. But I don't as it means more time away from the family. The bus is most uncomfortable, but I am getting a little used to sleeping on it. I have been trying out some meditation apps on the phone. They are relaxing, but I do feel a little stupid breathing in deeply over and over again in public.

The American Express Lounge now serves my favourite breakfast ever in an airport. The one in Stockholm is located in the restaurant *Pontus in the Air*, airside at Terminal 5. Since I have the privilege of having a card that gives me access, I order the full cooked version with simply the best scrambled-eggs in the world. It is far better than the other lounges that I have access. As mentioned before, I have not gained enough points as yet for the Star Alliance Gold lounge. And I don't fly business in Europe as it is pointless. But little perks are always worth it. It makes the air travel more bearable.

This is the last time I shall be flying to Norway. I had booked this trip months ago, and at that time, I had not looked into the train option.

Oslo is only three and a half hours away from my house. To fly there, I must first take the bus for three hours to the airport in Stockholm. This is also in the opposite direction. Then, since I must be there for at least one hour before my flight, I must take that into consideration of doing nothing for that hour, apart from the usual security lane queue and lounge breakfast. The actual flight path is over my house to Oslo and takes about one hour. Then I land still one hour away from the centre of the city by car, which must stand in line to hire. So what could be a three hour drive is in fact a six hour tiresome slog.

My hire car is a Volvo v40, which was different. And nice. You don't get this sort of car usually. Well not in the price group I order. It is more common to have some rubbish from car manufactures you can't pronounce.

I liked the way I could connect my phone. I liked the seats. And I liked the way it moved. And it is genuinely a nice place to be. I have to do about 500km while I am in Norway so this will eat up the miles.

On this trip I am to visit a football stadium in the outskirts and also some golf courses in the north part of the city. So one night in the suburbs of the city sounded like an excellent idea. Having not explored this part of Oslo and thought it would get me in more of the locals view I booked a Thorn Hotel and was very pleasantly surprised. I had gotten a good deal, and thus the hotel was extremely good value. The rooms were large and business like with the stationary set out on the desk. The bathroom had both a bath and a shower together with white fluffy towels.

I found a nice little bar and restaurant close by which was quiet and served a good selection of food and beverages. I enjoyed the space in my hotel room with a glass of wine and an episode of a television series I am following.

With other customer visits further South of the Oslo city, I booked the P-hotel. It is located in the city centre near the Parliament. On checking in to the P-hotel, I notice the lobby is a little small. Somewhat similar to the cupboard under your stairs to be honest. Still, it looked relatively clean and as I looked around, waiting in line two things dawned on me. Firstly was that there was no restaurant or bar. This is not usually a problem as I tend not to eat in expensive hotel restaurants anyway. But the lack of these most basic amenities did worry me on the quality of the rooms.

The second blob of disappointment was that there was a terrible looking fridge that had some yoghurt and Scandinavian half-finished sandwiches covered in plastic sitting there. This means that there is not even a breakfast room. Now, this had not popped into my head previously as some hotels have these rooms on different floors so one should never judge a hotel by its entrance. Disappointed and quite angry with oneself, I received my key and went up to my room.

Note to self: always look at the photos of the hotel before paying for it.

The room I have looks terrible. Old and outdated. And it was not even that cheap. I left it and went in search of dinner. I did not want to stay in my room any longer than I needed to. I found my usual place in Oslo and had some whale followed by a pork knuckle. On my way back to the hotel, I passed by a sports bar and popped in for a last drink. On the basis, I had no call until 10 am I thought it was ok to have a few beers. I started to chat with a Finish guy who was in town for a conference on computing or something. He suggested we go around the corner to another bar. Fine, why not, I certainly did not feel tired and not being in my room was fine.

Now A karaoke bar is, in my opinion, odd. I had not been in one since I was in China. Anyway, my new friend ordered a few beers, and we sat down and watched a few terrible attempts. I could not stop myself from taking the piss out of every single one of them. Now I know I can't sing. I have no talent on this or any other musical matter at all. It does not stop me from having an opinion on others who also cant. If you can sing you have my respect but if you can't then don't think that a few drinks later you sound like ABBA.

I left just after he had sung some Take That song and I could not sit with him any more. It was only about midnight, and that was good enough for me to hit the bed and check out of the hotel the next morning as fast as possible before my customer visits.

I am woken with the banging both in my head, and the wall just outside my room. There was also some sawing, hammering and sanding. Similar has happened to me before in San Marino. I needed some water, and I needed to get out of this place fast.

With a McDonald's breakfast on the move, I completed my calls for the day and headed up for the hour drive to Tyrifjord where I was to see Ian and stay overnight at his house in Hønefoss. Even though he had planned a whisky evening, I was going to be taking it very easy. I had some early calls to do and did not want to be over the zero alcohol tolerance that is Norway.

The week was coming to an end. It had been a successful week being able to see almost everyone I had planned to visit. I was about to enter a ten-week straight travel time that would take me all over Europe starting with Portugal, and the sun-kissed city of Lisbon. This time I would get to do all the things I had planned to do back in January and did not.

23. Lisbon September 2019

The reason for this trip to Lisbon was to join in the Greenkeepers Association golf gathering just south of the city. I had met some of them in the Algarve meeting, and now I was to meet members of Lisbon region. This being a golfing event I was to meet up with one of the organisers at the event the in the morning to pick up some clubs and get introduced to the members before hopefully not making a fool of myself playing golf with a few of them.

I did, however, have both an afternoon on my arrival day and an afternoon after the event for myself. The flight cost was cheaper to stay two nights than return on the afternoon after golf. And this time I wanted to visit a few places and experience this city, albeit around my work time. I would bring the Ipad with me and would conduct my work from the walkabout of the city in true digital nomad style.

It was on this trip, and indeed in preparation for this trip that I thought that if I am to write a book on my travels through Europe, then I may as well go into a bit more detail and inform you, the reader, of places that you should visit or avoid. I know I have mentioned bits and pieces in passing through these chapters, but I will say that they are an afterthought. So From now on, I shall give you more detailed information regarding restaurants to go to, and avoid. Hotels to stay and some to drive past. And also hopefully some cultural past or even history of places that I have the fortune to visit while visiting bits of Turf around Europe.

So far, I had really only got started in my role as a European Sales Manager. I had kept up my original direct customers in Norway, built a little in Austria and set my sights on developing the distributors that have taken an interest in our company. The coming weeks are to be the crucial ones, as we all know, it takes three years to make sales work and build the relationship. The first you scope out and speculate. The second is to develop and break even. The third one starts to make a revenue, and this is when it is essential to sustain the business for the future. The relationships get more robust, and trust becomes stronger.

I had a standard early morning with an uneventful taxi and bus ride to Arlanda airport. It is weird that now I start to recognise people. There are the security guys, a few now I begin to say hi to. There are people in the American Express lounge that now ask where I am off to this week. There are also a few passengers on the early Monday mornings that I am sure I have seen before.

With a connection in Zurich and the plane having a delay in getting off the stand I was worried for another long wait in a Swiss departure lounge, and I am not sure I could do that twice in one month. But this being a travel day it was not so devastating to the work schedule as with no customers to visit I could work from anywhere, even Zurich airport. I was, however, looking forward to an evening of sightseeing in the sun-kissed city of Lisbon.

On arrival, it was raining. I picked up my hire car, which came with a name. First time for everything. It was an Adam and born into the world by Citroen. I quite like it. It is small, elegant and for the streets of Lisbon, perfect. It was even more in its element when arriving at The Barcelona hotel I find that the small car park was under it, tiny in fact. So Adam felt right at home all cosy in the corner next to an exceptionally good looking aged Alfa Romeo.

After check-in, and a shower to wash all the dirt from travel, I decide to go on a walkabout to find a rooftop bar with the best view of the city. I had discovered there were quite a few in the city, and the one I wanted to go to first of all was at the top of the Intercontinental hotel. I find the lift in the grand entrance hall and go up to the level just below the floor it was supposed to be. On opening the elevator doors I see that it is closed. Not to worry I had a list and the second rooftop bar, was located on top of the Grand Hotel not far away, and it was open. I sit there with a glass of wine and read my emails in the sun. Shortly into my second email response, an American couple ask if they could sit in the chairs opposite me. With a smile from me singling it was fine, they sat down and ordered some drinks. Not bothered that I was reading or writing they soon informed that they were on their anniversary of something special and could I take a photo of them with their drinks in the sun. I obliged, and after handing the camera back and sitting down, I picked up my wine glass just in time to be splashed by the woman almost falling head over heels in the pond. There were gasps of horror followed by much laughter all over the bar.

The pond is not that obvious to see, to be honest. I almost put my foot into it earlier too. It was virtually the whole length of the walled side of the Terrance we were on. I can only imagine how many people have put their foot in it, trying to get a closer look at the view from the edge of the wall.

Finishing my wine, I decided to go for dinner. I could not be bothered to walk any further into town as I had to get up very early and drive and I know me. I walked back towards the hotel and went in search of another venue on my list, *The Old Vic pub*. It was also closed. Not having much luck I headed for the hotel and found a quiet looking restaurant called *Clubs do Pixe*. I was hungry, and it looked ok, and on closer inspection, it was full of motorsport pictures. A little lost in translation, I ordered some fish, and it duly arrived relatively quickly it has to be said. It turned out too quickly. My monkfish was cold, and when they took it away for replacement, they just nuked it, badly. For me, you replace it and start again, but I guess this was not MasterChef. Anyway, the wine was fine, and I left with no tip and went back to the hotel to bed.

The early morning drive to the Portuguese Greenkeepers Education Day and golf competition was about an hour. It was a beautiful drive over the water on one of the great bridges that span the river. With even more fantastic views of landscapes and rural Lisbon, I arrive at the golf course. I must have walked lots because the golf I played was shit. I lost all the golf balls I am given by my fellow players. The presentations were challenging to understand as they were in Portuguese, but no matter, it was the people I wanted to meet.

After the presentations and meeting some new people we parted, but not after making plans to meet at the annual conference in November.

The drive back was excellent, and Adam was great to cruise with. I decided to take the other bridge option and my god I am glad I did. With the sun high in the sky, it was amazing to see just how big Lisbon is. And the airport is right smack in the middle of this sprawling city. My flight out the following morning was very early. I had no other option due to the costs of the flights. I must keep to a budget, and it was cheaper to stay in a hotel for an extra night than fly out today.

The plan for the evening was for another epic walk, try some sardines, jump on a tram and go up an elevator. Ditching Adam back in his underground car park I quickly changed and grabbed my satchel and in it my iPad, a book, a water bottle, and a few other things I might need for this long walk into the city centre, passing the rooftop bars of yesterdays treks.

Getting closer to the city centre you see more and more tourists. And there were many. I found one massive group all hanging out of a sardine shop. I joined in and bought some tinned fish to take home. Famous for its sardines these shops offer hundreds of choices. Not keen on sardines, then you could have rare oysters, urchins or other fish and crustaceans, all stuffed in hugely elaborately designed tins. It was cool and felt like I was shopping in a fairground.

Happy with my purchase I fancied another tradition of this beautiful place. A Tart. And not just any tart. A custard tart with an espresso sidekick. This combination is simply a triumph of flavour. A perfect pick me up and an absolute must if you are visiting.

I was glad I had taken the time to get some sustenance as the line for the Elevador de Santa Justa was huge. After waiting patiently for an hour to get on the lift, We slowly lift to the top. It is an old lift by architect Raoul Mesnier du Ponsard who is forever closely connected to Eiffel and is beautifully designed.

The view is fantastic, and worth it. However, when you get to the top, you realise that you can just walk around the block uphill and discover no line or wait. Still, this is what I am here for. To give you the info you need not to do stupid wast of life things as I have.

I had a beer and enjoyed the view. But there were things still to do, and things to see. Next on my list was the "Ginjar" drink made of cherries. Very nice and only a euro. You pick them in microbars all over the city centre where older men pour the sticky stuff in shot glasses. You get a cherry or two in also which you are then meant to spit out the nut or kernel. It was late afternoon and not wanting dinner and not having lunch a snack it would be. Walking a short while uphill, I find I am close to another place on my list of visitations, the square that was the beginning of the revolution in 1974.

Walking down towards the waterfront, beautiful monuments are waiting for you as well as thousands of restaurants that look very enticing. Finally, I hit a big square where, oddly, the museum of beer is. But I have to say it was not the first thing that caught my eye. It was "The Sexiest Toilet in the World" sign. Needing the loo, I popped in there. Paid my euro and yes it has many pictures of men and women in little clothing. It was clean. Oh, and the toilet rolls are multicoloured. Worth spending a Euro, I think. Sexiest maybe not, but certainly the most spotless public toilet I have ever been.

I stopped in the square for another little delicacy, a codfish cake.

The fish cake is very small well worth it. I don't mean to sound glutinous, but it is a national dish. And perfect with beer it turns out.

Did I forget to mention the Russian? I backtrack. On top of the elevator on the viewing deck, there was this Russian girl. She was probably late 30's I guess with her under ten years old daughter. Wearing a white long tight evening gown and posing everywhere and even getting what can only be described as her household staff member to take the pictures of her with pouting and breathing in. She was good looking, but I am sorry there is only one reason she did not have a ring on her finger. I don't think any man would satisfy her for more than two days.

I digress. Back now to the square.

The sun is beginning to set as I sit here now wondering what to do. The time was getting close to 8:30 pm, and I had walked miles. I set my sights towards dinner. I wanted to walk along the banks of the river and I checked my map app.

I had planned to have it in the *Time Out* market. A big market where you can pick many different options from many different counters. The *Time Out* market was about 30 minuets walk along the river so this was perfect. On arriving there, I took a seat at the main bar in the middle and ordered a glass of wine to enjoy while scoping the place out and people watch. Within seconds a woman sat down next to me and started to talk. She was Irish but lived in the States. She continued to interrupt my thinking and people watching and inform me of her life, her travels, her children, and then asked me if I wanted to go back to her hotel. Yes! This is true! A 66 years old woman was pulling me. I politely declined and left the *Time Out* building with no dinner in slight disbelief.

I was heading back towards the centre of town. Still laughing at the visions of what the night could have been, I grabbed dinner in restaurant near the elevator. I ordered a pork belly with spinach, and it was terrible. Second dinner in a row that I ordered the bill before I had the plate removed. I shall make sure next time that I do a little research on the food side as I am sure this is not representative of Portuguese cuisine.

I jumped into a taxi and went back to the hotel. The foyer and the bar area are filled with most of Singapore. I started talking to one of the guys at the bar. A very well organised holiday is what they were on. It turns out it is the simplest way to get things done. I picked up my water bottle from the barman and headed to bed.

Checking out of a hotel before they serve breakfast is not something I recommend. It is dark, and although the drive to the airport is about ten minutes, I needed to find fuel and check-in luggage. And being a German airline, I assumed it would leave spot-on 7 am.

Failing to find fuel or someone at the hertz office, I dropped the keys in a box. I am sure they will charge me for that, but I could not have gone around it would have cost more to get a new flight.

Having gone through security and walked the standard winding walkway through the duty-free shop making sure you see all they have on offer I found a coffee. With just enough time to drink it, I took the 20 min walk to the gate. Sitting next to me was a massive guy in a bright blue suit who must have had a terrible hangover. He popped out various sugary items and water. He was sweating and not looking on top form, and when the food trolly came around, he refused the cooked breakfast. I had the nuclear hot breakfast, which I thought was nice for airline food even though it was hard to tell what it was exactly as it was so hot.

The connection in Frankfurt is always, for me, quite tricky. After walking the entire length of Frankfurt airport, I reach the connecting plane just in time for the short flight to Stockholm. I was looking forward to another meal onboard since you get food on airlines in mainland Europe. But just as we took off, we were informed that the food option for the economy class had not been delivered to the plane so we could only have drinks and a salty packet of something.

I look forward to revisiting Portugal, I wish I could stay longer and find a really good restaurant. Maybe next time.

Next week it will be Estonia and a conference I shall never forget. With a good blend of people on the attendee list, it would be a good one.

24. Estonia October 2019

I meet Lee at Stockholm airport. He had only just made it from his connecting flight from Manchester and we were booked on the same flight out to Tallinn. We caught up on things and looked forward to the conference we knew very little about.

We had planned to meet with Russel at Tallinn airport to share the taxi to the hotel but had missed his connection in Copenhagen and was put on a more interesting divert via Riga, before landing in Tallinn late in that night. Lee and I laughed at his situation and said we would let him know where we were going to be so we could grab a beer together.

Lee and I took a short taxi ride into the city and to the hotel. Checked in and dumped our bags and immediately went in search of a drink and other delegates. On our walkabout I got a little sidetracked in a gift shop full of tat where I purchased a box of matches for my cupboard of shit with a picture of President Putin on stating that Moscow "does not believe in tears". We walked towards the old town where we found many tourists taking pictures and the large town square. We took a few pictures ourselves of the magnificent surroundings and buildings and then found a cave that served beer and ordered some. It was dark and quite romantic so after just the one we left and not far away we stepped into a beer hall, which was much better. We had a 1L beer and discussed what the conference was all about. We had not visited the associations' meetings before as the association was quite recently formed. Neither of us had much information, but we knew it was to be a day full of seminar discussions and meeting Greenkeepers from the surrounding clubs.

I had arranged to meet with customers and friends from Sweden and Norway for dinner, so I checked with them and invited Lee too. We found the restaurant called *Leib Resto* and had a sumptuous meal of soup and quail. I highly recommended it. And the wine list was not too shabby either. I can always rely on those guys to find the best eateries around.

We then headed for another bar where we were to meet with some of the others and the organiser of this event.

A few drinks later, we headed back to the hotel. It was late, and we needed to be up for the start of the Estonian Greenkeepers education day.

Breakfast at the Tallinn Hotel was lovely and covered all the food angles. I would have described the hotel in more detail, but to be honest, it was merely a business hotel, minimal character, and nothing to write home about. Seeing some of the others huddled around some yoghurt, I grabbed a bit of fruit and coffee and joined them.

The coach drive to the golf course was to be about twenty minutes, and we are greeted on arrival outside the very impressive clubhouse. This, with its panoramic view of the course and sky with the Baltic Sea in the background was impressive. It certainly was up there with some of the best.

The day started with coffee and then an introduction by the course superintendent, who also happened to be the president of the Greenkeepers Association. It was to be an interesting day.

I wouldn't say I criticise other companies, or their sales guy. In fact, I don't, it is a rule. And I stick by it. I think it is downright unprofessional to rubbish another's product line.

However, when I am fronted with someone who rubbishes what I do and how I do it with the products I sell, then that person is not someone whom I wish to waste any time over. I endured listening to rude comments about everyone else's products, with the occasional piss-take from my customers that I just sell drugs. It was very awkward.

Back to the hotel on the bus, we decide to have a quick drink before showering and getting changed for the organised dinner. Lee ordered and got a bottle of brown for Russel, an almost full beer for himself, and a glass of wine for me, which was slammed down on the bar top nearly shattering it.

It was a short walk to dinner though the old town of Tallinn where we ended up in *The Ames* restaurant. It has a medieval setting and with live music from small people stuck on perches in the corners of the restaurant. As it was medieval themed, wenches served us a fantastic three-course meal. I mean excellent food, with some of the guys having Elk, or Moose steak for the first time. Unfortunately the authentic beer we did not enjoy so much, and finally, I got wine in a stone jug which was simple and basic table plonk.

Now, as we were to leave, I thought it only fair to meet the sales representative for the competitor fertiliser company that was sponsoring the dinner. I thanked the representative who was picking up the tab, and to my surprise, he almost immediately started to comment that my customer, standing next to me, should buy off of him the following year instead of me. I was speechless. Here I am thanking a guy for dinner and he tries to poach a customer in front of my face. A simple rule in not how to sell! According to my customer, he has well and truly closed the door with him. Forever. Ha!

I was a little angry at this rudeness, so we moved on towards the beer hall where Lee and I had enjoyed a litre the previous day. Finally, we left and walked back towards the hotel where quite a few of the other delegates had gathered after dinner.

We ordered a few drinks in the lobby bar, and I chatted with various customers on the happenings of the day. At one point one of the female Head Greenkeepers described how she was experimenting with types of liquid feed.

"I go squirt squirt in each test cylinder and wait the results" She says.

I fall about laughing. It might be my mind but In describing this I finally get out a few words between laughing and breathing

"That is now your nickname, Squirt Squirt".

We all have a giggle and agree that forever more she shall be know as Squirt Squirt.

Having got to bed quite late, the sleep quality on my phone had reached new lows. According to the App, I had only had 34% good sleep. It felt like it if I am honest, but at breakfast, we discussed the day to come. I was not going to play golf, but I was looking forward to the course walk and finding out how well the course was headlining their method of greenkeeping.

When the education morning and non-existent course-walk came to an end we hitched a ride to the city with a local fertiliser distributor. Lee, myself and Squirt Squirt went in search of lunch before Lee and I had to catch our flight back home. Bouncing my bag down the cobbled streets of the old town, as is usual for me, we found a lovely cafe and sat in the petite window section with our coffee. Squeezing in we waited to see if Russel could find us. It was a little entertainment whilst we enjoyed a warming cappuccino. Judging on the previous evening of him not being able to take any directions or the simple ability to read a map we thought it would take some time for him to find us.

He did eventually find us, and we went for lunch. The taxi ride to the airport was brief. I like it when airports are actually in the city for which you are visiting. The Toyota Prius Taxi was driven by its driver like it was stolen. He must have hated it so much. I don't think he used the hybrid bit at all.

The airport is small but efficient and very easy to navigate around. Having being stripped at security Lee and I tried a few local hats on in one of the four shops. We then played some table tennis for a while.

Why do they not have more games like this in airports around the world? It is such a brilliant idea. I even broke into a sweat as we got more confident with our shots. It certainly was better than sitting on a rubbish chair drinking. I mean you are there to get a seat on a plane so why not get some exercise in before you do. The game ended when the ball landed and gently rolled around the crotch of guy relaxing in a massage chair.

With Lee on his way and myself not being able to find another partner for more exercise, I sat down and had a coffee before my 45 min flight back to Stockholm.

Next week a trip to the Head Office in the UK. I shall be stocking up on cheese, sausages, and Jelly Tots. All things I miss so much in Sweden.

25. UK October 2019

Taking 12 hours to get to my brother's house on the South coast of the UK, the travel day is a full iPhone battery length. It is incredible how much work you can do if you ignore where you are. What I mean is that if you get stuck into whatever you are doing and that your work is mainly computer-based it is possible to work a full day, and even more by simply ignoring the world as it goes by. You just move along as required by the travel. Relocating and opening up the iPad or Laptop and carrying on as if nothing had happened.

Arriving in Bosham, my brother and I immediately went out to the pub for some real English beer and a packet of pork scratchings. Simple things I miss in Sweden. And anywhere else I happen to be really. Don't get me wrong. I think that Europe has wonderful food and beverages, but there is always something or a few somethings that gives you a sense of where you were born.

On the London train from Bosham I notice the morning commuters of the pre-six am train services in the UK have many things to distract them from their horrid start to the day. I noticed that the local rail company had used up some valuable advertising space to let everyone know that the doors would close just before the train leaves. And that if everyone could pile on faster, their train could run more smoothly and on time. I noticed this while waiting for my delayed connecting train in Guildford. Reading the metro newspaper, I notice the countdown to Brexit advertised. It informed their readers to get ready with more information on the Government's website. I needed something for the shelf of shit, and it is now together with my nodding British Bill Dog in Union Jack clothing and a copy of *Five on Brexit Island.*

It is great to catch up with everyone in the office and also pick up my amazon deliveries. Having had an all-day sales and marketing meeting, my colleagues and I all jump in whatever vehicles are available for us foreigners to have a lift and head to our overnight pub stop. *The Royal Oak* in Yattendon, as previously written, such a perfect pub. Set in such an English garden, but it has one flaw, and that is it's plumbing. It is terrible to bring up the mad concept of having a separate cold and hot tap again but blend that with shit plumbing then you are going to have an exciting shower for sure.

The thing is *The Royal Oak* slams that negative to the ground with its excellent food and atmosphere, and on this occasion, it was no exception.

Sleeping well in the deep soft pillows and duvet the morning was started with a proper full English after drying myself from the shower in the huge white fluffy towels. I can't complain.

I had a few hours to kill before my taxi would take me back to Heathrow for my flight back to Sweden. With the week in preparations for my next trip to one of my favourite cities of all, Prague.

26. Prague October 2019

I needed to see my customers in Prague, and I was looking for the opportunity to get a visit in before Christmas. One of my customers had put in his first order for the coming year, and another had started to work with us, so it was essential to meet them, even if it was to be a tight schedule and only one night.

I had also really wanted to meet with the distributor that we had there at the same time as they were due a visit to catch up and I needed to introduce them to our new range of products in for 2020.

With not such an early morning, I was around to wake the children up and see them off to school. Even though it is a small amount of time, it does make the trip away feel less, how does one put it, away!

However, I realised that we were running very tight to make the bus I had booked from Orebro City to Stockholm Arlanda airport.

My wife and I got in the car, and we raced like hell. Not passing over any speed limits at all. In the city, my wife and I had three sets of lights to get through, and everyone hit the red. Finally, we slipped into the parking, and I got out, kissed Lina goodbye and ran to the bus stop where the bus was not.

The bus arrived a few minutes later than was scheduled to and then I had another worry, really wanting to be with the children for breakfast that morning I had only left 45 mins to get through security and board the plane. Even though I have access to the fast track and already found out the gate number, it was going to be tight. I arrive security to find that there were no boxes on which to place my bags and coat. Then there was the standard idiot who had so much stuff in his pockets directly in front of me. I still don't understand this. And before I digress into a rant about morons who travel with no respect for others, I shall move on. Myself all prepared I get through with no problems I walked up to the gate and right onto the plane. Perfect.

Landing in a terminal new to me, I follow the signs to the hire car pick up point. It was good to find out that it is 2 km away from the terminal. Not really, but it was certainly a long way away from the terminal 2 that I had landed. Very quickly, I receive my keys and get the sat-nav set up on my iPad. The car was a brand new Skoda Citi car which was terrible. And blue.

First, stop was to Jordan at his course that had not yet fully opened. Having not seen the new workshop set up, and the spectacular golf course for what it is, Jordan, took me on a long drive around the massive property. We had made plans to meet with two other course managers, Ben and Tom, later that evening also to have a good catch up and discuss how things were to work for the coming year. I was supposed to go to one of these other courses later that afternoon, but it was getting too late in the day to have a meaningful visit. We put it off until the morning.

Driving back into Prague City, I hit a little traffic, but it was straightforward to find the hotel if I am honest. I had not driven in Prague for several years, and after getting a vague idea of where I could park my gutless blue from the hotel receptionist, I find a spot easy enough and it was very cheap. It was not to be as cheap as I found out months later when I would receive a €30 fine for parking wrongly somehow. A full overnight parking spot is one-quarter of the cost of other major cities, without the penalty obviously.

My hotel was simple but clean and tidy. The Three Crowns Hotel in Prague is just outside the main city centre but still walking distance to everything. The connection via tram and bus also is extremely good. I ordered my two tickets from the reception to get into and out of the old town. And after a quick shower, I head into the old city. I walked along the bus route and finally missed one between stops. But on the basis the cost was so little it was pointless to stand and wait, and I like the walk anyway and I know my way quite well through the streets of old town Prague.

Dinner with the guys was excellent. We found a new place, and it was memorable as our waiter forgot our starters of jalapeños. I must also mention that when we ordered our meal, the cheeky little waiter suggested that myself and Tom, may wish to have a whole duck and not just a quarter that was on the menu. Not that we are that large we found slightly rude but still funny.

After dinner, the guys suggest *Hooters Bar.* Now I have been to *Hooters* in America, and it isn't very good. The waitresses are dressed up or should I say dressed down. It is not really my scene. I shall say that the bar, as bars go in Prague, is terrible. We left very quickly.

Arriving at the golf course the following morning where Tom worked. We walk around the unopened golf course, admiring the fire bushes surrounding in perfect contrast to the ponds water edge. And what a clubhouse, massive and it can be seen from miles around.

I left there and went for the drive through the city to my final golf course visit the European Tour course where Ben is. It is always such a privilege to call on this one. We had a reasonably quick drive, though, and I took photos and headed back to the workshop to go through new products for the coming year.

Dropping off the hire car, I walk the 2 km from the airport to the terminal. At check-in, I am offered an upgrade and was looking forward to the lounge, and a free drink, and lunch. It was not to be as

SAS does not have an agreement with the lounges in Prague and only Gold Star Alliance members have access. I grab a quick beer and boarded shortly afterwards. It is such a pleasure receiving an upgrade and then having nobody sitting next to you. I had the salmon cube lunch option with some sort of dried apple thing I honestly can't explain stuck in the lid. I discover It also came with a small dill liquid-filled sachet which when I opened it the contents squirted all over my phone and shoes. I would have been better off in economy class. I did, however, take two of the free Swedish whiskey bottles and popped them in my bag to enjoy that evening when I got home.

Next week I am off to Linz to give a presentation to a bunch of Austrians.

27. Linz, Austria October 2019

For this trip to Austria, I was unable to book my usual taxi. So the new taxi company, worried that they would probably not find the house, turned up 30 mins early at 3:15 am. Instead, of being content with punctual timekeeping, he decided to call me, waking me, my wife, and my daughter in the next bedroom too much of our irritation.

It was a silent trip to the bus station, I find that thankfully the bus had arrived early. I would have been irritated if I not only had to get up earlier than planned but then had to wait at a cold bus stop in town. I found my seat, slipped on my eye mask and went to sleep. I wake up 15 mins before we arrived at Stockholm Arlanda Airport. I had used my accumulated points for an upgrade on my flight. It's not that you get more legroom, bigger seats, or better food. You don't. It is that I am very close to the next level up on the tier program, and I need to gain a few extra points. Thus using points to upgrade weirdly earns you more points and therefore pushes you closer to the goal I wish, fast track, and SAS Gold lounge access.

Today the trip takes me to Frankfurt airport, for which I have only ever been at to swap planes. I then would fly on to Linz in Austria. I have not been to this City, and nor will I go there either as I am to pick a car up and drive an hour north towards the Czech border and to the hotel and spa resort that we have the Austrian Greenkeepers annual conference.

Getting onboard the plane a guy pushes in front of the line and then is sent back as he was not a priority traveller, why do people do this? Get back where you belong! I am reminded of my "yellow" airline flight to Sweden earlier in the year.

At Frankfurt airport, I take the long walk between the F gates and the A gates. It feels like the full length of the airport. Onboard the aircraft, the usual security information is given, but whilst it was happening I was watching the confusion outside with the man operating the robotic machine that moves the plane into position out of the gate. It had broken, and clearly, it wasn't easy to replace it smoothly. Even though neither the captain or the stewards mentioned not a word of this, things just went on as usual. I continue to watch the situation from my scratched window. The broken robot is replaced by a new one ramming the broken one out of the way.

After 45 minutes in the air covering the exact amount of time to listen to two chapters of David Cameron reading his book to me, we land in a very foggy Linz. It is a small airport, and I walk around the hut containing the hire car desks. Naturally, I am welcomed with an upgrade, as everyone is who has ever hired a car. This time I get a Skoda something. It was blue and not very interesting, so therefore not much of an upgrade in my eyes. But then I had no idea what the car I was upgraded from was.

The Spa Hotel Brundl is located in a small village called Bad Leonfelden, on a hill, naturally in Austria. It is tranquil and since there are two large hotels, both of which were spa retreats it must be popular as a getaway spot. On arrival at the check-in desk, they cannot find my booking, but we finally found it and my room was great, the furthest away on the first floor. Being the corner room meant that I had a lounge living room area in a sort of triangle shape. The shower is simply outstanding, and the shelves were full of fluffy white towels.

Having refreshed, I call one our distributors who was also attending. Three of our distributors were to participate with one of them giving a presentation on the second day. Frank answered but was clearly on his bed relaxing. You know you can tell. We made a plan to meet in the lobby bar and catch up and for him to give me a better idea of what to expect at this event.

My German is rubbish. But I can order drinks, which I did. We chatted, and I am introduced to a few people who were his customers. Frank fills me in on various attendees, who were with what company etc. I asked if there were many Greenkeepers or Groundsman that he could see around the bar. He pointed out that for most, there were trade reps. Unfortunately, this is common. But I hoped that this would change as not everyone would be staying in the hotel.

The evening is enjoyable with dinner being an extensive buffet of what I actually thought was very good considering. As I am to be giving a presentation on our agronomic services the following morning, I decide to go to bed. I prepare myself for the presentation, looked over the slides and fail to go to sleep. I put David back in my ears and finally go to sleep. I am woken with nightmares of the presentation failing and having to take deep breaths. I am not sure why I am so nervous. The presentation itself is not very long. I guess about 20 minutes, and I know the material well. After lying in bed for half an hour, I get up and smoke a cigarette on my balcony and watch some deer grazing around the hotel.

It is 3:50 am. I have watched the BBC news and caught up on all the Brexit issues of the day and quietly commented on Boris's actions to myself. The time was getting closer to five now, and I thought that if I don't go to sleep now, I will not bother.

I don't usually get nervous, well not very much anyway, and you must get a little bit as it puts you in the best frame of mind. Too relaxed and you miss stuff out. I was probably nervous because it was about 100 people, and I was the only one to be speaking in English.

I looked around the room for coffee and tea making facilities that are so normal in hotel rooms. I have hardly ever use them, but this time I had nothing. I did have a fully stocked mini-bar. I looked and thought, NO! I remembered that my daughter had suggested an app that she likes to listen to before going to sleep, a type of meditation. Why not, let's give it a go.

It worked, and my alarm woke me up at 7:15 in the morning, and I was tired. I slowly went to the shower and then went in search of coffee. Deciding against breakfast, I have coffee and coffee and coffee.

Still shaky, I went into the seminar room and tested the iPad with the projector set up. With technology and I working well, I sit down and look over the notes I had made on my phone. I planned to have my phone on the podium thing with me and take a slow start to explain who I was, who the company I was working for was, and what they did. I would be fine. I knew the content of my presentation very well. I should be able to do that.

I sat at the front and listened to the opening speech, then the first two presentations. They overran which was fine as we had a break before mine. I had a cigarette outside, looked over the notes once more on my phone and went up to set my iPad up.

The room filled and everyone started to sit down, I grabbed the mic, which was useless anyway and then realised that my phone was on the chair. I had no notes! I started the slides. And at least the easy bit was to talk about myself. The company bit was also easy. But I still had no notes and some great points I wanted to make it all to flow into each topic. Taking a breath, I pushed forward and looked at the presentation slowly. I think it probably went better than what I felt it did, but I still felt embarrassed. I was heating up. Finishing off I took some questions and answered them in full detail, that bit was brilliant.

The chairman of the Greenkeepers Association of Austria came on stage and thanked me for presenting, and me with a large box of produce from the local area. I looked at him oddly, since I certainly did not think I deserved it for a 25-minute talk.

Leaving the venue and back to Linz airport, I notice that the car had a sticker in the upper corner of the windscreen stating that when it is fitted with winter tyres, the max speed would be only 190 km per hour. I thought this a little excessive. Still, the drive through the clouds was fantastic. Such a great view on such a great road. The Skoda came alive on this road, and I thoroughly enjoyed it. I met with some of the machine sales guys at the airport and discovered that we were on the same flight to Frankfurt. We chatted and apart from me leaving my iPad on the plane and having to run back to get it embarrassingly, the trip home was relatively uneventful.

Next week it is to be the UK and a massive trade show in Birmingham.

28. UK Birmingham October 2019

Five am, and I find the airport very busy. Busier than I usually find it at this time. Being a Wednesday, and not a day I typically travel on I ponder the idea over a coffee of why so many people are up early to take a flight.

The walk to the bus that would transport us to the aircraft is on the far tip of the airport. It is the first time that I am flying into both Birmingham and the IOG (Institute of Groundsmen) show. It is merely a walk from the aircraft to the National Exhibition Centre where the event is taking place.

On arrival, I immediately meet up with some colleagues only to discover that one of my meetings has been cancelled. Quite annoying as I had spent the time and company expense on getting to this show for it. Still, I had a few other essential meetings, and thus not everything was a disaster or a waste of time.

One of my meetings was over lunch—a tricky thing to have nice at these events as the catering is basic, and the staff are stressed and not what you would call skilled. Thus the lunch was terrible.

Finishing off my meetings at 3 pm I head to see a British colleague with some of his larger customers. They had been in the pub for ages. This was relatively standard at these events where the sales reps pick up the tab for budding clients. I bought a round of beer and joined in for a chat. I was waiting for my train to London, so it felt like the perfect thing to do. I was to be there a while as my train is first delayed, then cancelled and then delayed again. Finally, I get on board and find my seat next to a man who could not stop eating pork scratchings. He went on for three stops before finally leaving me in a cloud of pork rind smell. Thinking this was bad enough, he was replaced by another guy who decided to open his train snack of bacon fries. The smells were lingering in the carriage until we hit London.

After my pork enriched train from Birmingham I had to zip through the London Underground to catch a train from Victoria to the South coast. I am thankful that I don't have to commute to London every day. I am not keen on the hustle and bustle of London's underground. It feels dirty in comparison to other European underground transport networks, but I wish not to complain. The system is a fast and efficient way to get from North to South London.

With another two-hour train trip from Victoria to Chichester, I went into one of those expensive train station shops to grab a drink and some snack. I came out of the shop with a glass of rosé wine in a can and some Jelly Tots. At Chichester, my brother, Dominic picks me up, and we go straight to the pub for steak night. It is so brilliant and amazing that they can do it for so little money. We do not have it in Sweden, and I miss it very much. £12 for a great steak and a glass of wine.

Just making the train to Gatwick in the morning, I arrive in time for breakfast. I had an easy trip ahead of me. Next to me on the plane is a sizeable chap who oozed into my space. It wasn't easy to get the iPad out to work, so I ended up working on my phone. Something I have not done and I am surprised how easy, when pushed, you can complete so many tasks on such a small screen.

Next week the UK, Portugal, and Bulgaria. Which I am sure it will be fun and with only twenty hours in Sofia I shall do my best to see some of it.

29. UK, Portugal, and Bulgaria November 2019

This week is to be a hectic one with my travels taking me to three different countries spanning one side of Europe to the other. All starting with the first snowfall at home just to make the roads that little bit more fun at 4 am in the morning. As the coffee percolator just about finishes, I receive a text from the driver of my taxi. I message him back stating that I shall be outside with him in five minutes. I will have a coffee with no exception, and he is 15 minutes early so he can wait in the car.

This taxi I had been in before, and it is one of the new models of Mercedes. The coloured led lights inside the footwell, the doors, and the roof, all give the feeling of stepping inside a video game. We zoom into Orebro, and he drops me off with 20 minutes to wait for the flight bus. I see that the coffee shop is open opposite and since this is not my usual silly o'clock start I take the opportunity to get a cappuccino to enjoy onboard. It is freezing, and I mean freezing. The temperature had dropped over the last weekend to below zero. Winter was undoubtedly coming quickly.

I upgrade my flight to London by using some of my Euro Bonus points. As mentioned before the more you use them for upgrades, the faster you earn even more points to gain the next tier. I am currently only one flight away from this goal with SAS and Star Alliance. And it has only taken since July to do so. Being the leading alliance of airlines I fly, it would become a very treasured travel accessory.

Having the rubbish cube of lunch on board the flight, I focused my plans on getting to my brothers for the overnight stop before my actual reason for travelling this week, the flight to Portugal for the Portuguese Greenkeepers annual conference. It was to be in a five-star resort on the Algarve, and I have to be honest, I was looking forward to it very much. It is not often I get this sort of opportunity.

I am to be picked up by Russel from my Dominic's house for our trip to Gatwick. He has a terrible sense of direction, but we made it none-the-less. I always find Gatwick a second level airport for London. Heathrow for me, is business with a sprinkling of wealthy holidaymakers off to Luxurious countries with their matching Tumi suitcases. Gatwick is, well, the poor little airport for those who are off to some hideous place where they don't serve anything local as not to upset the tourists. The terminal is full of people who have woken up one day and discovered that their lottery ticket had upgraded them from Ryan Air to British Airways. Not that BA is a luxury airline anymore anyway. The biggest mistake they did was to aim to be the same as Easy Jet with drinks and snack purchases onboard. The only difference is that the products you get offered to purchase are from *M&S*. Anyway, I now hardly ever fly them, so it does not matter. Sitting in *Starbucks* coffee house and enjoying a cappuccino when I spy a couple travelling with two stuffed penguins. They probably wanted to take them somewhere warm to an all-inclusive sun lounger. I was trying to think of witty comment to write about them, but if I am honest, I can't. Everything I do write is cruel so I won't.

I have just read the previous paragraphs and realise I sound so snobbish to holidaymakers and Gatwick, and I apologise. I guess with the number of flights and airports I spend my days in I want it to be smooth. Since I think I am the most important person in the airport I look at people like they have no head when they are in the security section and have not removed their belt or taken their coins out of their pockets before they enter the security pod. I know I tut at people that slowly walk through the endless unwanted route through the duty-free shop. Again I apologise if I offend. But why must we be forced to do this I don't know. When coming downstairs in Gatwick look for the sign to gate 10 as you reach the bottom. It points to you to go right. This takes you in a long-winded route around the escalator you have just come down, so you get the opportunity to see more shops. Why? The fact is if you just turned left, then you will be at the entrance to the gates you need. I hate it when we are guided by force to see products we don't need.

Anyway, we arrive at the gate and boarding commences reasonably quickly. I follow some happy drunk guys down the corridor to the aircraft with a blow-up man and find my seat. It is going to be one of those flights.

The flight was nice and smooth. I had nobody sitting next to me, so the extra space was wonderful. I caught up on my emails and listened to more from David Cameron.

Arriving in Faro when it is off-season is nice. It is quiet, and the hire car I had ordered cost less than 10 GBP for two days. Not bad, and certainly cheaper than a taxi. It turned out that the Fiat 500 I ordered had turned into a horrible Peugeot something. So with Russel as my navigator (Ha Ha), we hit the road following a truck that was delivering fish. "Capitao Iglo" to be precise and the logo was an exact copy of "Captain Birdseye".

Russel had not been to Portugal before so I suggest, since we had time, that we go to Vilamoura town harbour for a sunset beer before heading further down the coast to our conference hotel. The harbour was less busy than last time I was here, and we enjoyed a pint over some people watching.

The Pine Cliffs resort is massive. We parked the car and walked through the entrance to find it a good ten minutes away. We checked in, well, I tried to, but I had no reservation. I could see that it had been paid on an email confirmation, but there was no reservation for me in the hotel. And it was fully booked. Thankfully, Joel, the organiser arrived at check-in, and within two minutes, I had been given an upgrade to a suite. But I did have to sit in the bar and wait for the whole set up to be completed. This was not much of a hardship for me. By this time, many others attending the conference had heard of my upgrade, and I had one lady offered her room to me so she could have my upgrade. It took me a nanosecond to decline her kind offer, and I went to the bar to wait.

Almost finishing my wine, I am met by the manager and then introduced to a porter, who walked me to my room. He informs me of the history of the hotel and its buildings before we arrive in the Ocean Suites part of the hotel complex. Just as we got to my room door, he informed me that had put my bags in another room on a different floor and that he was going off to collect them and bring them down while I settled into my Suite.

On entering my Suite, I discover it is a standard hotel room. I have a desk, shower, toilet, double bed, tv, an empty minibar, and a small sofa and chair. I am not complaining as it was fresh, clean and very tidy. But it is not a suite I am sorry to say.

I went back to the entrance lobby to meet the rest of the delegates. They were gathering in the bar area before we are to head to the restaurant on the other side of the complex for the opening dinner.

The whole complex is designed for you not to see any bit of Portugal at all. They keep you in so you spend all your money there. There is even a jeweller who sits in her little shop, smoking and offering wine to passers-by to make them part with their cash. With the hotel filled with Greenkeepers and Groundsmen for the Annual conference, it is unlikely that the jeweller would gain much business from us.

The opening dinner is simple, and the food was excellent with many local delicacies and copious amounts of fish, with a few welcoming speeches rolled in. I get together with our distributor and a few others I knew. Later that evening, after dinner, we all gather for some live music in the bar. With the conference starting early in the morning it would have been stupid of us to carry on.

The conference was interesting, and there are many demonstrations and presentations that I would not like to bore you with. At the designated lunchtime we all float down in unison to one of the many swimming pools for an extensive photo shoot. As is so common with these events, it isn't easy to gather many people in one spot for a photo. After many attempts, it is done, and a large buffet lunch is laid on offer in return.

With the afternoon session relatively quiet in comparison I take the opportunity to catch up with some work in one of the cafes and later that afternoon I thought it would be rude to miss the chance to go to the beach. I discover the elevator down the cliff. I opt to take the stairs down through the cliffs to the beech. Beautiful as it was. The sun was out, and you can see why so many spend their holidays here.

The evening is to be a formal black-tie event. I don't understand this if I am honest. The industry that we work in is not a suit and tie industry. The working men and women of turf do not wear their Sunday best daily. They wear workwear. The salespeople also do not wear suits. We sell our selves, but more importantly, we sell our company and its brand. We all have similar clothes cupboard. Usually this will consist of a coloured t-shirt or shirt with the company logo, sometimes a jumper or fleece, again with our companies logo all over it. If we had suits, then I could only see the tie as a logo option, and this would be terrible. It would also not work for the women of the industry either. So why then do we, at these events, have an evening when we must dress in suits and ties that we don't usually wear?

At dinner, I add a new member to the Turf Travels WhatsApp group. He sells some bunker lining, and his name is Neil Diamond. No, that is his real name only spelt slightly differently, and does not sing. So with speeches over after a delicious final meal, I hit the sack early, leaving my fellow delegates, Russel and Kneale to enjoy an evening of live music and flowing drinks. Disappointed I missed the singing but this week is only halfway done, and I had to leave from Faro at 6 am for my flights to Lisbon, London, and finally across the whole of Europe to Sofia, in Bulgaria.

Flying TAP from Lisbon to London I notice I have an iPad holder on the seat in front of me. This allows you to watch things and not use the table. Or use the table for food, drinks, or snacks. Unfortunately, it does not work for the large iPad Pro. But still a most excellent addition to the seat.

After the third flight of the day, I arrive in Sofia, Bulgaria, and I am to be met by one of the board members of the Bulgarian Greenkeepers Association. I had no idea what he looked like, so I hoped he would have a sign with my name on. I look all around the arrivals area and then decided to go outside for a smoke and wait for him to call me.

I notice a guy wandering around the entrance where a number of us are smoking. He was holding his phone with a large picture of me on his screen. I introduce myself, and we head towards his car. I wonder where he got the photo.

He is to take me to my hotel where I would meet my Slovenian distributor, Uros, who is to be assisting in the region to both support our product sales and expand his area. The drive is a short 15 km drive to the hotel according to my map app on my phone. The traffic though was something out of a nightmare. Solid bumper to bumper traffic moving at walking pace. It takes an hour.

Arriving I have a speedy turn around since we are now late and we had a dinner booked with the other delegates across town. This meant a little more traffic, but first, I needed a quick toilet stop in my hotel room. On first impressions, the room looked quite acceptable. I opened the door to the bathroom, and the door handle fell off in my hand. Well, what did I expect for less than 50 Euro a night? After a quick re-attachment, I did what I needed to and met the others downstairs. I was getting hungry and wanted a glass of something.

Dinner, how can I explain this- it was meat with potatoes and an awesome dumpling thing. There were giant tomatoes also. Everyone was quite tired, and it did not take us long to consume it all like animals. As fast as the dinner went down came the beers flowing into the room. We had a few, and they were local and incredibly good. I wish I could remember the name of them.

The morning is difficult to wake up after such a long previous days travel and a relatively late night. I made it downstairs to meet our host at 7 am, unlike Uros, whom I woke up by phone.

En-route to the golf course where the conference is to be held, we pick up the translator. She squeezes in the back with us. We encounter more Sofia traffic, and I watch the city pass. I must revisit it. It feels a little halfway between Turkey and Italy, with a bit of Greece thrown in.

The golf course clubhouse is elaborately decorated, and the chair and table set up are similar to that of a wedding reception. But there is coffee and about 40 Bulgarian greenkeepers and groundsmen all waiting for our presentations to start.

Presenting when you have to pause after every sentence is difficult. You lose the rhythm that you may have in delivering, and it is hard to make it engaging. In the end, the presentation was fine and since I believe that the translator did not quite understand everything that I said it was ok. I was not the only person to have the use of the translator. A fellow Englishman, Ben from Ipswich was up next to talk about his club and how that is maintained. It was an interesting presentation, and Ben too enjoyed the translation at the end of each sentence.

After the presentations, we are offered good spread for lunch, but I have to leave the conference early as it was getting close to the time of my flight, and the traffic only just got myself and Uros to the airport. We parted company as we were to depart from different terminals. I stood in line for passport control. The line moved very slowly, and it was beginning to worry me. Eventually, the dodgy looking woman who had held us all up is let out of Bulgaria, and I am allowed through without as much as a second look.

Whilst at the airport I go to find something for my cupboard of shit. I try to do this everywhere, and this was a new country and city. I had not had the chance, and just in case I would not come back, I had to get something. About to give up and buy a local drink, a fridge magnet catches my eye. It was in the shape of the country depicting the flag, some monument of sorts plus a picture of the president. I thought it would it would look good next to my matches depicting Putin holding fuel pipes.

So to sum up my visit to Sofia, Bulgaria; well, it had bumpy roads. The smog is terrible, and the city is expanding so fast it feels as buildings go up in the time it takes to have a coffee. There is certainly money, and with golf courses getting more popular, and more money is being spent on them, the interest from companies like the one I represent becomes greater. We as a company became lead sponsors for the Bulgarian Golf Greenkeepers Association I shall certainly be back. And I shall take some time to explore this wonderful country.

With a change in Warsaw, I flew Polish airlines for the first time to Sweden. And I think it would also be the golden flight for me with Star Alliance. It is a small plane; Embrerra 170 to be precise. It has good size seats and a very large table. Much better than the flight of the day before. And another difference was that you get free coffee onboard.

With only one full day at home, Italy and Slovenia call me for the next week of my travels.

30. Italy and Slovenia November 2019

A Sunday start. With only one day at home leaving the family again was not nice. I could see the end though, and the long time from December until Harrogate in the third week of January. A break from travel most welcomed.

Sunday travel should not happen. But it occasionally does, and one must fulfil what one has as a goal for the year. I wished to visit all of the customers we had all over Europe, and even open up new markets, and then adjust in the coming year according to some sort of priority and then manage that.

Among many things to do on a plane, watching sport is quite common. Mostly I have witnessed people catching up with football, motorsport and tennis. But the man sitting next to me on this flight was watching squash. This I, and I may be alone here, think that this is an odd sport to watch. It's a bit like watching lacrosse but faster-paced. The man is getting excited, and I found it hard not to smile. I focus on my book, but it is hard not to look over myself. Maybe once you have watched squash on TV, it becomes like a drug. You wait in anticipation for one of the players to splat themselves into the wall.

With a very short stopover in Munich, I have just enough time to get to the other side of airport grab a smoke and then jump on the bus to the aircraft for the short hop over the Alps to Venice. It was the first time I am flying with Air Dolomiti. It is quite strange that the aircraft seating is set just perfectly between two windows. So you end up pushing your face to the window forward to find you are cheek to cheek to the passenger in front. But then you lean back to you find the opposite situation with the passenger behind. I wonder if it was one of those moments when the interior designer had just finished installing all the seats, getting an extra two rows in above his brief thinking he would be rewarded, only to then see the problem and say

"Shit!, Oh Well".

At Hertz, there was no waiting at all to pick up my Panda. I like Pandas, you know it has no power, but it does show it in a style I like. The drive to the hotel takes about 2 hours, and it is raining. This is when you know you are in a Panda. The rain battered the windows and roof, and at one point I think it might just break through the glass.

I can't quite remember where the hotel was. I know it was at a golf course, but my notes fail me.

At the hotel I eventually locate the parking and meet with a few people that I think I had met before, we chat and then I check-in before for a terrible dinner for one, parting with an extortionate amount of money in the basement restaurant of the hotel. There was nothing around the place at the venue, nothing to explore, nobody around, and nothing to do. I decide to take an early night with a movie. My Italian distributor, Edgardo, is to meet me in the morning, just before the show. This is to start at 9 am, and we need to set up our stand.

Like many of these shows, it is full with mostly trade delegates, but Edgardo and I have an excellent chance to catch up, plan and go through products to have in his portfolio for the coming year, and generally get to know each other more. During one of our conversations, I discover that he covers France too in his sales. And since I was looking for a French distributor, it made sense that he cover France as well as Italy.

It is the afternoon, and it is getting quiet, not wanting to hit the bar we both decided to remove ourselves from the stand to return to our rooms to catch up with some emails and calls. It is a busy time for me with many different places to visit so any time like this is a golden opportunity to have some quiet concentration time, keeping in touch with customers in other countries that have seen or will be in the coming weeks. Good communication in this job is a must.

The dinner is an elaborate affair with cocktail and nibbles set out on a buffet and then a main three-course menu on the tables. We are situated in the clubhouse of the golf club. The room is quite basic and has little character. With no set seating arrangement, I sit with Edgardo, his colleague, and a few other Italians that ignore me. I try to start a conversation, but it was fruitless. I delved further into the wine and had them each described by Edgardo.

I stayed until about one o'clock with people who now had the confidence to speak to me in English as they had lots of drinks inside them.

I received a text the next morning from Edgardo. He had packed up and left as he thought it was not worth staying longer. I walk about a bit and then head off for my three-hour drive to Slovenia for their greenkeeper conference. Two in a week is tough going.

I had been unlucky not to get a room in the hotel where the conference was to be. I had therefore booked a hotel at a reasonable price some walking distance away from it. On arrival, I found that I had booked a very nice hotel. It was the first hotel in Portoroz, and it was massive. It was old, but the experience of staying at a Kempinski hotel is not something one should ignore.

Firstly a man meets me and suggests that he may go and remove my car from the front of the hotel where I had parked it. Obviously, it was not good enough to be with all the higher-end vehicles. He suggests my Panda should be in the garage.

Then a woman asked what drink I would like while I wait at the interview style check-in area. I check-in, and during this process, am given a history lesson of the hotel and the surrounding area. I quite liked it. The man then suggested he take me to my room. I denied him this. It was too much. I am capable of handling my bags in a lift to a room.

I dumped my roller bag and emptied some stuff from my shoulder bag and decided to walk in the pouring rain to the conference hotel about 2km down the road.

Soaked, I arrived and sneaked in for the final two presentations of the day.

With ten minutes left of the last one, I slipped out with Lee and went to the bar. We caught up a bit and are joined by my distributor Uros, wearing a new colourful hairband.

After a few beers, Uros and I leave and head off to our hotels to get ready for dinner. We had both been unfortunate not to get a room in the conference hotel.

My shower had a rail perpendicular on the wall like most, but the water tube with the shower-head connected to it only reached a fifth of the way up. I found this uncharacteristic, mainly because everything in this hotel was of an extremely high standard, but how someone installing it could walk away pleased with their work I am not sure, nor I could imagine the line of managers who missed this error in the installation.

Anyway, I knelt in the bathtub to wash my hair and then stood up to wriggle around the jet stream with my lower body.

In the lobby I wait for Uros to pick me up. Dinner was not a sit-down affair but a networking event. This is fine, and the food was good. I met new people and hopefully new customers for Uros and myself. This conference has a reputation for attracting neighbouring countries delegates in the sports turf industry to attend. It is one of my favourite conferences.

It had rained so hard during the day that the smoking area outside was blown to one side. The weather was so bad that we heard on the news that Venice was flooded with a high tide. And the airport where some were flying from was also affected.

Uros, Lee, and I joined a table, including Mike, a guy who works for a competitor of ours. There were also some representatives from a Czech distributor that our company uses. The conversation went on, and I noticed that the only female in the group was wearing a t-shirt with the print "Rafiki" on it. I pointed out that it means "friend" in Swahili, but she did not believe me. Not joining us, Rafiki went to bed as she had a long drive the following morning back to Prague. We all went out. It was now quite late, so there was not much open.

The taxi we had ordered from reception took us first to the main casino, which was too complicated to get in and dead, and then he took us to a strip bar that was open and willing to serve a beer to two. There were ladies there, not that we were interested in that. It turned out that of the three, one was not "working", and the other two were just grumpy. We sat at the bar, and the conversation must have gotten deep as Jeremy, another fertiliser salesman and indeed a turf traveller, fell asleep at the bar. We have photographic proof and it occasionally gets shown about. He blames age but we think it was beer.

I remembered that another one or our turf travels little group was coming in late from Denmark, where he had attended the Danish Greenkeeper conference. I called Kneale Diamond and checked where he was.

Not far away it turned out, so I suggested he stop by, have a well-deserved beer and then drive us back to our various hotels. He agreed and we gave him directions leaving out the bit about the strip bar.

Leaving, we see the taxi driver that had brought us asleep in his car, presumably waiting for the only customers he was to have that night. We got into Diamonds Mini and went to the hotels to bed. It was 4 am.

The following morning was tough to deal with. But I drove up to the conference hotel to do what I was there to do, work. With some of the talks not relevant to me, I caught up on emails in the lobby and joined the rest for lunch. Some delegates had left earlier to catch flights, and as the weather was not great, I don't blame them. Some had snowstorms to drive through. We found out that this little town had also been the victim of this water surge. We had not noticed from our intoxicated state.

Lee and I had booked the days a while ago before the conference organisers had confirmed it all, and with our schedules, it makes sense to do this, we can't wait until the last min to book. So we had ended up with an extra night. It meant that we had the evening together for a wander about this small coastal part of Slovenia.

Meeting up just before the sunset, we walked the length of the waterfront. We found nothing apart from one of those boards with an amusing picture on and the hole where you put your head in while someone takes your photograph. We did that and then decided that a beer would be a good idea.

The town was so dead. I mean there was nothing, and Lee and I were struggling to find other people and a busy place to join in and have some fun. An Irish Bar perhaps, because that would have been perfect. We discussed while we walked that no matter where you go, you always find an Irish bar. Anyway, there wasn't one, and we did not want another late night anyway.

Having walked the whole length of the coast, we looked at the map whilst haven't an Aperol spritzer in a dingy little bar with us as the only clients. We decided that we may as well go further up the coast in the other direction and go to the point where you can see

Italy and Croatia whilst standing in Slovenia. There must be a restaurant or bar there.

We walked into a nearby hotel and asked the concierge to order a taxi for us. It arrived in two minutes and was the one that we left outside the strip bar the previous evening. A little embarrassed we got in and whispered about giving him an extra tip.

We arrived in the main square of Piran. We walk around the cobbled streets, muttering on how Russel would be struggling with his ruined ankle and complaining if he were here. We wandered further, looking for a place to have dinner. We found the point where you can see the coast of Croatia and Italy, and we saw the castle and a nice collection of boats. But again no bar and not a lot to choose in the food department. There was one dark-looking place where a few old guys hung around one place drinking wine and smoking roll-up cigarettes We carried on and in the end, decided upon a pizza joint. Not taking card payment we left there immediately and found a little further down the road a romantic looking restaurant. It did take card payment and was at least filled with some people, albeit masters student on a party night out.

We had a wonderful dinner, fresh fish and a steak, not bad for very little cash. Still tired from the previous night's escapades we order our taxi guy back to meet us in the square where he had dropped us.

We wished each other a good weekend with our families and confirmed our meeting plans for the coming week. Lee was to meet me at Malaga Airport and drive us up to the Spanish Greenkeepers conference in Almeria. It goes on!

31. Spain November 2019

The taxi company are certainly getting used to me and where I live. At 2:30 am, my alarm wakes me for what was to be a long way to Malaga.

After my usual cocoon sleep on the bus to Stockholm Arlanda airport, I arrive, zip through security and have an enjoyable breakfast in the American Express lounge.

My flight to Oslo is slightly delayed incoming from Oslo due to heavy snowfall. I liked the comment from the captain

"The runway is slippery with heavy snow, please put on your seat belts".

Hopping he, being a Scandinavian pilot, could handle this. I planned my route out of this plane and onto the next. Whilst taxiing, I informed Lee by text that I might be late or worse miss the next if I cant get to it on time. I would let him know when I get on board. I did not want to miss him as he was to drive us both up to Almería for the Spanish Greenkeepers Conference, a few hours drive from Malaga.

So it put a little pressure on me to catch my connection to Malaga. We arrived at the gate at the boarding time for my next flight. Thankfully, the gate that we arrived at and the gate of the next flight was a 5-minute walk. So I walked off of one Airbus and immediately onto the next.

With that stress over, we sat on the stand for the next 30 minutes waiting for our turn in the de-icer part of Oslo airport. The snow was heavy, and we finally left 30 minutes after we were supposed to.

The flight down to Malaga is about three and a bit hours from Oslo, and it went smooth for the first hour. Then the flight attendants called for a doctor on board. This is the first time I have witnessed this. You see it in movies, but now I have been in that situation. Not being a doctor, I just watched to see how many of my fellow passengers were doctors. A person had passed out or something. I noted that we immediately dropped in altitude and then the captain, shortly afterwards, suggested that we may have to land in London to have the medical team to attend to the passenger. After a short while circling the north of London, we were given the go-ahead to continue to Malaga, with the doctor regularly checking on the individual.

On landing, we are delayed, and there was a medical team who swiftly dealt with the ill passenger. I zipped through the airport as I knew that Lee was waiting for me. As it happens, he had gone to the train station to pick up a guy called John, a groundsman in the North of Spain. Originally from Scotland, he has morphed his way into Spanish life, speaking perfectly fluent Spanish. Also, with a claim to fame. He was the bagpiper at Seve Ballesteros's funeral. A great honour, I am sure. I found them in the express car park, and we headed for the 2-hour drive up the coast and on a beautiful road to Almeria. The coast road is quite something. I am not sure what the name of it is but oh my word it has breathtaking scenery.

On our way, we stop for a late lunch. Food is in a different time zone in Spain. Lunch starts at three in the afternoon and dinner at nine. It is not unheard of to have desert after midnight. Anyhow, I order a beer and squid salad, and it was perfect in every way. We are to wait and meet another guy who is developing a microbial product for our industry. I know him now as Paul the Microbe, an Irishman living on the Spanish Coast. He is very tall and has massive feet. So the name seemed to fit him perfectly. He is a man full of stories.

Back on the road, we split, with John and Paul the Microbe in one car and then Lee and I in the other.

I had not been able to get the same hotel as Lee, or the others and had booked a cheap room in the city. With him dropping me off, we made our plans to meet up later that evening with the others. I checked in, took a shower and unpacked ready for my three-night stay. It is weird to write that, but it is true. I don't often stay in one place longer that one night, two at a push. So three nights in the same location will be strange.

I popped into the hotel bar to find out it wasn't the hotel bar. It was merely a bar next to the hotel. It was a very locals type of place, and I liked it. I had a plate of tapas cheese and ham and washed it down with some wine. Being late, 9:30 pm, I debated to meet up with the others. I ordered another wine and then decided that I should. But being awake since 2:20 am I did not think that I would last very long.

I was to be very much mistaken.

Walking down to a bar on one of the many high streets and found John and Paul the Microbe sitting smoking and having a beer in the beautiful evening sun. I join them. Soon Lee called and suggested we meet him and some others at the *Mini Bar* on a side street not far away. We went there, and it reminded me of the bars in Portugal where you pick up the cherry liquid so delicious and light, yet addictive. But in this case, the *Mini Bar* serves you a small glass of beer. They also served us a plate of freshly grilled prawns, and we had two.

Moving back to the original bar Paul the Microbe left. It is 1 am and leaving the three of us with many Spanish Greenkeepers and Groundsman. I was amazed I was still awake.

The bar closed at 3 o'clock. Not being smart in any way at this time we jumped in a taxi and headed to another bar. We played pool, and I have no idea how I could see the other side of the table. I finally arrived back to my hotel at 5 am. We had discovered at some point in the night, or it could have been morning, that Tuesday was to be the setup day and registration. There was to be a themed opening dinner in the evening, so I was picked up by the Microbe and John to go to the congress centre about 20 mins away, just outside the city and passed the airport.

We could not find it at first, but eventually, we did. I registered and picked up my passes and tickets for the dinners. We hung around for a while, speaking to delegates and then decided to get another lunch on the beach. We are joined by two wonderful people, who work for a large turf nursery supplying turf all over Europe.

On the way to the restaurant, we stopped by a Chinese shop to pick up a USB Stick for Lee for his presentation tv on his stand, and I bought a donkey for my shelf of shit. A terrible little ornament but together with the Cowboy hat and my plastic Sherriffs badge, it would remind me of this trip.

I should mention now that the evening theme dinner location was to be the location of the Wild West movies and Indiana jones etc. The venue is called Fort Bravo. We had initially been to the Chinese shop actually to buy some toy guns. But since that would cause far too much hassle on the return flight home, we decided not to buy them. Oddly enough whilst looking at our options, I received a message on the Turf Travels WhatsApp Group and Kneale Diamond was asking how the Spanish show was and was it worth attending. I send him a picture of us with toy guns stating we were preparing for an evening in fancy dress and thus picking up supplies. He responded with some worried comment.

At the restaurant, I can't remember the name of it, but it is just passed the end of the Almeria airport runway, we find a great rustic looking spot outside. We chat away and finally give in and decide to check out the fish bar inside filled with a beautiful selection of animals of the sea. The food is so fresh it is hard to describe.

John and Lee had to go back to the Congress area for a meeting, so Paul offered to drop me back at my hotel so we could have a rest before the bus was to leave his hotel and take us all to the desert Wild West mini Hollywood set.

After a freshen up I still felt tired and not fully recovered yet from the previous night's entertainment. Regardless, I walked the 15-minute walk through the city to meet with the other guys and jump on our bus. On the way I stopped by the bar we were in the previous evening to see if Lee's coat was still there. It was not. He was to suffer then. He had lost it before, so clearly there was some underpinned hatred of it.

To my delight, we were all given cowboy hats sponsored by some turf company. I attached the Sherriffs badge and got into the mood by sending a selfie to the Turf Travels group.

On arrival to the Fort Bravo set, we are ushered to the centre square. I don't know what it would be called, but if it were a modern city or town, it would be the square. There we offered frozen beer and some crisps whilst watching some scene where a baddy is thrown about, shot at, thrown off the top of the jail, put in the jail, escaping from the jail, shot at again, dragged and finally hung. He then got up and took the applaud.

During this, some horses ran at high speed with men in leather shooting in the air. It was exciting, weird, but entertaining, and it was cold. Especially for Lee just in a light checked shirt and no jacket.

We are herded, like wild west cattle, into one of the many rooms or buildings and we took a table with the same guys as we had at lunch. We could not have been more closer to the loudspeakers if we tried. We were then entertained at extreme sound volume by live music from a duet. It was of a standard slightly better than karaoke level, let's put it like that. It was, however, a level higher than that of the food, which was dished up and then taken away shortly after being moved about the plate. It was not good. We commented that we might see some of it later.

Having a headache, I went out for a walkabout on my own through this film set. It is eerie. I liked it. I smoke and walk, absorbing the atmosphere. I join the guys again, and we were herded up again across the dusty town centre to the saloon bar where we are to be entertained with even more free drinks, and some can-can girls. They are outstanding. If you have ever watched "White Lines" then the first episode is filmed there as well as movies like "Indiana Jones" and numerous American Westerns.

On the way back to the hotel, Lee jumped on with us city dwellers as he assumed we were all going to go out for other drinks. But being almost 1:30, none of us are up for it.

The town was dead. I had the feeling that everything was going to be closed, but since the bar from the previous night was on my way to my hotel and feeling sorry for him, I said I would join him for a beer there. If it was closed, then he could get a taxi back.

Lee complained about the lack of taxis all the way from where we were dropped off only to discover the entire city's collection of taxis were parked outside the bar.

It was open and filled with Greenkeepers and Groundsman. And some rather attractive ladies it has to be said. We sat down, the only ones with our cowboy hats on, and ordered a beer each.

Four beers later and meeting and mingling with a number Spanish football Groundsman we moved from that bar, with the girls, to a dance bar around the corner. The time went by and soon it was 4 am, and the congress was to start at 10 am. We called it a night.

The next morning I took a walk down to meet with the Microbe and John. I did not feel hungover. I was ok. But I was tired. At the congress, I was to meet with my distributor from Portugal. We had to go through some things and make a few plans for the coming year. I saw him on the way in so we peeled off and had our meeting.

With that sorted, I was on a mission also to find a distributor for our products in Spain. I walked around and spoke with many people. And think that I was to be successful in achieving what I wanted. Time will tell.

The Turf producers stand was the busiest. But I think this was because they had wine and fish all over it. I joined in trying out some odd-looking dried fish. Wonderful. Washing it down with a late morning wine felt wrong.

Towards the end of the days show I got my usual lift back with the Microbe to my hotel. With the evening proceedings starting at 9:30 pm I wanted a shower and a rest. I had some emails that desperately needed doing as they were essential quotes. So I finished with them and slept from 7 pm until 8 pm. A very weird time to have a nap. I felt groggy to say the least when I woke again.

I was also in a position where I had to organise transport to the airport the following day. And I had to leave early too. So there was no way I was going to have a late night again.

After asking numerous people for a potential lift with no luck. They had afternoon flights, and there was no way they were going to give me a ride at 7:30 am. Eventually, I had found an app that provided the best prices and also it gave a vast selection of options of transport to choose from. There was budget, luxury, business, comfort, bus, and a helicopter option. I chose budget and booked it.

I walk down to the other hotel to meet the guys for a pre-dinner drink. The dinner was to start at 9:30 pm and for me that is far to late. But you do what you have to do. I drank frugally too.

My plan was to leave the event immediately after John had received his plaque for being Groundsman of the year 2019, he had been told that he had won in advance for some reason and I wanted to be there for the celebration and to congratulate him properly. I knew that if I stayed, it would be too much and too late for me to function for the long day of travel to come. I left just as the desert arrived at midnight.

The taxi to the airport was smooth, and I slept quite a bit of the way there. Onboard the Airbus I find the "delightful" passenger in front of me had his seat fully reclined. He continuously laughed laughed like a monkey jumping around when his fellow passenger sitting next to him spoke, so whilst I was typing up my expenses and notes for this trip the seat and my table bounced around everywhere. Eventually, the child is told by its parent to sit down and was then given a screen to look at.

Next week Iceland.

32. Iceland November 2019

This trip to Iceland consists of the last four flights of the year. However it is my penultimate trip of 2019.

It all starts with a lost taxi. I did make it to the flight bus, but only just. With this being my first outward gold star alliance member flight with SAS, I wanted to see what the fuss was about in the SAS lounge and particularly the 'gold' members-only section. I can report that it is the same but with fewer children. Mostly suits if I am honest. I had been itching to experience since July and it turned out to be a massive disappointment. I have been invited into the first class lounge at Heathrow and there is a significant difference to the silver lounge. I had a Scandi breakfast and headed to my first of two flights for the day—this one to Oslo.

In Oslo, I walked the vast distance of about 30m to the gate next to the one I landed at and waited for five, maybe ten minutes before being first on the plane! On the basis, the flight to Oslo I was second on I wanted to see, as a new gold member, if I could trump it. I did, and now I don't care any more.

For the 2-hour flight to Iceland, and more specifically Reykjavík I was lucky enough to have nobody sitting next to me. Keflavik Airport is about an hours drive south of Reykjavik itself sitting on a peninsular with views over the cold Atlantic Ocean all around. There is very little else there.

I pick up my hire car and remove the thick crystals of ice from it. I drive directly on road 1 to the capital, Reykjavik. You can't get bored of driving here. It is beautiful, simply mesmerising. I wonder how many crashes are caused by people in wonderment of their surroundings. How did your accident happen? The view out of the window just blew my mind!

The hotel I have chosen for this trip is situated in the centre of the main street. I had walked here the last time I was here. It is close to a few bars and most of the restaurants that were more frequented by locals and tourists alike.

Checking into the Sand Hotel, I find my room clean and truly Scandinavian in it's crispness. There is no restaurant but a small bar and coffee shop which doubles as a breakfast room.

I decide to walk and find some dinner. There is a pub and restaurant that serves beer and soup. The vegetable soup arrives in a bread. Literally, and it is incredible. I do not feel like a massive meal, and it is cold, so what more can one wish for than a piping hot soup in its own warm bread.

A couple is sitting next to me, and I can't keep my people watching eyes off of them. The older man has been to South Asia and brought a girlfriend back, who is a quarter of his age. But that is not the issue. Many mixed couples exist, including me, being married to a Swede; however, he has given up. Burping and farting throughout the meal. I am sorry, but it is disgusting, and I felt sorry for the woman. Maybe he could not help himself.

After dinner, I wandered back to the hotel and contemplated grabbing the car keys and driving out to a spot where I am told you can see the Northern Lights. I have seen these wonders before but in Sweden years ago but to them in Iceland would be something special. And the Aurora Borealis is one of the real sights of Iceland.

Well, I did not. I opted for a nice glass of expensive red wine and watched some rubbish on my iPad, then fell asleep.

Waking up at 6:30 am I get ready to drive and pick up a Groundsman, called Magnus, who was to be my guide for the morning. We spend the morning driving from one football stadium to another, Many are indoors, and most are artificial pitches. However, there were a few that were natural grass pitches, but they are covered in a very heavy frost, not quite like the major clubs in the UK. Here there was underground heating for the pitches, but since they were not in use, nor was the heating. The other difference to major high league pitches that I have visited is that the security was almost non-existent. Then again this is the country that knocked out England in a World Cup, and the Icelandic players have other, more full-time jobs to worry about.

After a lovely Thai lunch, we head to the Icelandic Greenkeepers Conference. We have a few presentations to listen to, and I am to give one. This education time is to be followed by their Christmas Dinner.

On arrival, I meet one of Lee's colleagues, Richard, and we catch up and take the piss out of each other's presentations. After the presentations finish, we head down to the greenkeepers workshop, past the old tank where they held the Free Willy whale. Inside we are greeted with drinks and food. Since I was driving, I was sticking to an unusual local non-alcoholic drink and water.

It is strange to have a night out without drinking. At about ten, I said my goodbyes and wished Richard a safe flight. He had had a few and was having his distributor take him to a hotel. I drove back to the city and had a quiet wine before bed.

The flights back were uninteresting, and I spent most of the trip home working. With a full week again away next week, I felt that I could not work at all across the weekend.

Next week it will be back to Norway. The first time I take the train from home. It will be different. But it is also the last trip away of the year and that will be nice.

33. Norway Oslo December 2019

Travelling by train when I lived in the UK was terrible. You know it will be dirty, noisy, and not on time. Ordinarily, in Sweden, it is the opposite. The seats are significant, and it is clean with individual bins by each chair that are not full of chewing gum and so disgusting you can't touch them. They go on time, well every train I have been on has been on time. And they are quick and quiet.

So to find a text message to say that my train is to be delayed, and then another text about an hour later to say that it will be swapped for a different train altogether was a bit surprising.

I received a further text saying that I would be reimbursed 50% of the ticket because the wifi was not working. And then an additional 25% off the remaining 50% back because the breakfast was not complete.

If anyone were to complain about this level of service, I would be shocked. 50% back just because the internet was not available. This is brilliant.

The boring bit is that it is only part of my journey to Oslo. I am to take the train as far as the Swedish City of Karlstad and then the coach on to Oslo main bus terminal.

With a quick change from train to coach, I find my seat is directly above the toilet. It means that I can recline it fully without worrying about fellow passengers, but occasional interesting wafts of smell engulfed my nostrils from the what must be a full toilet.

It is a three-hour drive from Karlstad to Oslo. It would be mostly highway, but this is winter, and therefore the roads are icy or winter roads as more commonly named. I felt it was better to take the bus than my car. Plus leaving it for the family is better than me having it in Norway for the week.

Arriving into Oslo central bus station, it is only a short walk over the bridge to the central train station. I found the hire car machine with no issue as it is clearly signed and simple to use. I pick up my horrible little Lexus hybrid something. I try to connect the phone to its Bluetooth, but it is full and can't connect anymore. With no patience, I make a few calls I had to return. I wouldn't say I like speaking on trains or busses. Not because of whatever I have to say is essential or secret in any way, but because it is just very annoying for other passengers.

With a quick get to know your car moment I found the micro gear shift and I zoom off in silence. The hybrid bit worked until I got out of the car park, then it needed engine power. The roads were a little slippery, and I had to take it easy. At -9 degrees you never can be sure where the ice is.

Reaching my first and only call of the day I find both I am early and two, the warm workshop canteen area is guarded by a Labrador. Even though I know the dog's name, it growled at me but wagged its tail every time I said its name. Not that I am scared, but I was bitten by a dog years ago, and it is not pleasant.

With nobody about I call Duncan and John and then proceed to pass the dog and chill out with emails until they arrive.

Once we had gone through all our new products for the coming year and talked crap about various topics, we parted company, and I headed towards the city centre and my hotel for the night.

There is little traffic for a change, and I found the extortionate parking lot with ease. Grabbing my bags, I take the short walk past the statue of the finger-pointing-down made even more famous in "Top Gear's" race to Oslo.

Now I like Radisson very much. They are an exceptional hotel chain. But the budget version the Park Inn I like less. It is more compact, which is fine because you get what you pay for, but the showers need looking at. The glass protecting the water from filling the room is far too small and don't work. I used all of my fluffy white towels to soak up the water on the floor.

Heading out to one of my favourite places to have a beer in Oslo. A place where it matters not if you are on your own, and sitting typing up a book chapter on your phone. *The Dubliner* Oslo represents everything a fevered traveller wants away from home when they are tired. It is friendly and is as quiet or loud as you like to be. There are ample bars scattered all over this vast interior space. It has an enclosed heated smoking area which is rare. Here you are neither inside nor out, with all the heating lamps that cover the air space above to keep you warm.

I decide to order some Irish stew and a Guinness. They arrived, and I then remembered that I'm not too fond of Irish stew. I am not a fan of Lamb in the boiled way. I ate half and finished my beer. Ordering another beer, I decide to go back to the hotel room for an early night and also speak to the children on FaceTime.

I was exhausted. I could not stop yawning. It was only 8:30 pm. So the natural thing for me to do in this situation is to brush the teeth and go to bed, but did I? No.

What I did was go downstairs and ask where there are any exciting bars to go to in the near vicinity. So a glass and a half of wine later I meet up with a customer form a city golf course, and we head back to *The Dubliner* for a last drink. A whisky. Never a good idea.

With a massive headache, I awoke, showered and went in search of bacon and juice. Having replenished my body with nutrients and having paid the extortionate car parking fee, I hit the road to my first call of the day.

You might think that since the grass is covered with snow that we can't visit or do anything as sales reps, but this is the time of year that you get the real chance to speak to the greenkeeper. They have a little more time for you, and you also get to inform them of new products or go into more depth with their program plans for the coming year. And with the likes of Sweden, Norway, and Iceland ordering all of their requirements in one go for an early year delivery, one must have this time to plan.

My second call is cancelled due to ice. Well, more specifically, James could not get out of his driveway to get onto the non-gritted ice slope that is his road. We spoke on the phone for a while and went through some plans. I then decided that I would have lunch at the *Munch Museum*. Now at the time of writing the museum is held in a rather depressing building in the city. It will soon be housed in the fantastic looking modern building on the waterfront overlooking the amazing National Opera house. So it will be a cultural area of interest when it is finished in early 2020.

Whilst at the museum cafe, it would be ignorant of me not to pop in and see *The Scream*. I am here, after all. And parking was such a nightmare I may as well.

I paid the NOK120 entrance fee, bought a souvenir 3D eraser of *The Scream* for my cupboard of shit and went through the security control to get in.

I was in and out in ten mins. This is how you do it. See what you want to see and leave. Driving back to the hotel car park I decided that what I want to do more than anything right now is get out of the hotel, have a walk and find a cafe where I can both catch up on emails and plan a little for the coming weeks. I walk around the city centre and pass through the Christmas market. I love these in Scandinavia. I love them all over Europe. The real start of Christmas. I never buy anything in them, but I like walking through them. And the one in Oslo city is one not to miss. With giant Elk heads that talk to you in Norwegian as you pass and literally about one hundred stalls selling everything from whale meat to Spanish crepes for some reason. I tried a little smoked whale, contemplated buying a packet, thought against it and walked on in search of a cafe to work.

I sit in the *Sentralen Mat* cafe around the corner from my hotel. It is full of mothers with babies, breastfeeding. And the long stretched table in front of the window is lined with Apple Mac Laptops and iPads. All are working on product designs or books. It is so busy here that I am lucky to sit down at a table. I have discovered also it is part of *The Gathering of Similar Minds* at Lava Oslo. These chefs have a superb selection of restaurants, and I shall make sure I fall into this later for dinner.

Having briefly gone back to my hotel to freshen up, I came back out to test the *Sentralen* restaraunt. I must have missed the main entrance as I found myself in the main section of the restaurant and asking for a table for myself at the bar, which I am promptly told I should see the man at the properly defined entrance of the establishment.

On requesting a table for one, I am shown a menu in the way that he thought it was not my kind of place. I said that the tasting menu sounded very nice, and I would like to have a seat. He told me that because I have not reserved previously, I would have to be out by 6:30 pm. I explain that this was fine and he takes me to a table in the almost empty restaurant.

I sit down and look at the menu. Within five minutes, the place was almost full. It seemed like there was a show in the next-door building. Everyone needed to get some food in before.

I ordered the tasting menu of Norwegian aged ham with sourdough bread which also came with a mushroom truffle dip as one dish, the beef checks for another and to accompany it I order the pan-fried Sprouts. This also was to come with a dipping sauce and sliced something that was also excellent.

The selection of beer in the place is good and the wine too. I opted for beer based on the state of my body from the previous evening. I did not want any alcohol, but one beer with dinner would work.

I have often wondered what it would be like to be a food critic. I mean popping into restaurants four days a week and then writing about the food. I guess that it is part fact and part personal experience. Maybe I will go into the details more in the follow-up to this book.

So I have sat here reading the news and various other things and have just noticed that the time is creeping up to the 6:30 pm deadline. I must vacate the place, but not all of the food has arrived. I am looking forward to the beef cheeks. Maybe they are so small I must down them in one mouthful.

Service has been adequate to my liking in a semi fine dining restaurant. Now I am not sure how long is the norm to wait for the main course after the starter section. But twenty minutes I feel is too long. I am also getting the feeling that my waitress had noticed my agitation, and I think that she had a short chat with the head chef.

It turns out that my waiter at the beginning who wanted me out of here has had it all go wrong for him, my order was not given in correctly to the chef. An excellent plate of food arrived at my table, a hanger steak to be exact, and it did look good but it was not mine. I thought about eating it but it was not mine and I knew someone else would be very disappointed if I did. I want to have what I had ordered, the beef cheeks.

When the cheeks arrive I do eat them quickly, but the taste was ruined by the experience a bit.

The food was all exceedingly good, I cant deny that and I would recommend it very much. Quite reasonable for Oslo and about €30 for the three dishes. It was a pity that the service or communication was not perfect for that evening. Still, I will return for more.

After a good nights sleep, which was needed, I hit the road to my first call of the day about 45 minutes drive south of Oslo. The streets were incredibly slippery with light rain blending with the snow to make a nice compacted lethal surface.

After a meeting with my customer there, Steve, the iron man, I leave and head towards the tunnel under the Oslo Fjord. I have been on this road before but from the other side. You stick the car in cruise control at 80kph and enjoy being under tonnes of water for about twenty mins. It is truly a feat of engineering.

After about 40 minutes into the drive, I realise that I have missed the turnoff and was following the Sat Nav on my phone with no re-gard for where I was and not looking at signs. I find myself heading toward a port. Well, a ferry. I arrive at the port where the automatic payment is, I drive directly onto the boat with no time to change my mind or turn around.

I may have mentioned this before, but I'm not too fond of boats. I get seasick and avoid them at all costs. But now I had driven onto the thing, and by the time I had undone the seatbelt and opened the door, the boat was floating off.

I wandered up to the cafe on board and sat down to look at the view. There wasn't one. The foghorn was blazing, and the visual dis-tance was about 30m.

The water was, however, very calm and after watching the safety video and an advertisement to donate to the air ambulance, I went onto the front outside deck for a look at where we are going.

Getting off the boat was very simple and fast, and I soon find the I am back on the road towards my second call. Logan, a Scotsman there welcomed me and handed me a strong cup of Norwegian coffee. We chatted, and I brought him up to speed with our latest products. Wishing each other a good and joyful Christmas, and planning on meeting again in Harrogate in January at the International turf conference, I leave for my final call of the day an hours drive back up the other leg of the Oslo fjord.

The fog had settled in, and the viability was terrible. Driving became slow and horrendous. With the useless Lexus I had, I did not feel comfortable. I had noticed just now that it is called an F-Sport. I can confirm to you that it has a dial thing inside that you switch between sport and eco mode. The only difference is noise.

I arrive to meet with James. His dog licked the groin of my jeans and then my socks to welcome me. We sit down in the workshop, and I have another strong coffee. The usual procedure of discussing products for the club, we discuss the courses he manages and the plans for the coming year.

We quite often go out for a meal when I am visiting, but due to the dog sitting situation together with his very young child, this was not to happen. I leave and plan on finding an Indian restaurant for dinner alone.

After a fantastic meal at an Indian restaurant I can't remember the name of I go back to the hotel for a movie. Maybe I should not go into more detail for restaurants. I forget them often. I make a mental note always to collect a card or photo from the place I am eating in the future.

Waking up for breakfast I head downstairs at 8 am to discover I have another meeting cancelled so I check out of the hotel and head back to the *Cafe Sentralen* again to work. That afternoon I would head up past Tyrifjord Lake and the island where that Norwegian guy shot many people in a horrific attack. It is such a great road with even more amazing views but has a tragic history.

This final night away for work this year, I am not to be staying in a hotel. I am to stay with Ian. I always look forward to seeing him and his family. The children I have known now for several years. I always bring over some sweets and alike from the UK. This time I am coming from Sweden so they would be a little disappointed with the fact that I have just bought some presents from Norway for them.

Sitting at the window in the cafe, I join the line of Mac Laptops and iPads. Everyone is plugged in and typing away, occasionally sipping on their coffee.

The drive is slow and get stuck in traffic leaving Oslo city. Eventually I arrive to a wonderful home-cooked meal and happy children. As I hand over a few goodies to the kids Ian and I catch up. The stories continue over dinner, and it is nice to end the year travel like this.

After dinner, Ian and I get down to see work-related planning for the coming year and catch up with product info and updates as usual.

As the clock strikes precisely 6:30 pm a friend of the Ian, PG arrives, and we put the work away to make way for a whisky tasting evening. Both Ian and PG enjoy this, and so do I if I am honest. I don't drink spirits much anymore, and this is the only time I drink whisky now. I must be sensible though, as I had to get up early to drive to see Gavin, another greenkeeper working on a course near the airport. If time permitted I would also visit and Irish guy, Eoin before I must leave Norway on my train back home to Sweden.

The whisky evening is a success, and I learn a few more whisky facts from PG. I may not remember them, but he is a world of knowledge on this drink. We enjoy the drink, and they are so diverse in flavour.

After a strong coffee, some food, and a few glasses of water I head off to see Gavin. We have a good meeting and the usual sales conversations roll. With time pressing I speak with Eoin and we plan for meeting in Harrogate in January. I head back into town to Oslo train station. I bought a few things in the travel shop *MOW*, which was excellent and full of brilliant ideas and products to make packing and travelling better. This is the sort of shop I like to see. They should be in airports.

The train is smooth and enjoyable. I caught up on a few emails and then relaxed with a wine to end the week. Lina was to pick me up the other side and then with only a 15-minute drive home to see the children all is well. We would sit on the sofa and watch a movie together and I could not wait.

I lasted 15 mins and fell asleep.

With only a few weeks left of the working year and no travel my life slowed down. I would plan for the coming year, book meetings, and start all over again.

And so the cycle is complete.

PS.

I was going to stop this book here, but due to the Corona Virus Pandemic hitting the world it made sense to continue into 2020.

Firstly it felt that finishing this travel memoir made more sense to end in a European wide lockdown, but more so is the fact that there would be so little material for 2020 it would mean that the follow-up book would be very thin.

So into 2020 here we go, starting with Harrogate, UK as the first port of call for the British and International Greenkeepers Association annual conference 2020.

34. Harrogate UK January 2020

I am back in the UK after a well-earned winter break. Landing into Manchester Airport, I am met by one of our directors for the good drive to the hotel in Harrogate. As you may remember, it is not my favourite hotel, but this time I am greeted with the keys to the best room I have had when staying here. The shower is good with decent pressure and also warm water together with fluffy white towels; it truly is an upgrade on past stays.

The afternoon is full of meetings, and I have a discussion about Europe with the boss Carl. Afterwards, I meet more of the company team in the bar, and we all have some drinks and discuss how it is all going in our relative areas of work.

We have dinner, and after a few drinks in the local pub, I meet with Lee and two of my customers. We head towards a busy bar with lots of greenkeepers and groundsmen all very much under the influence. We catch up over a few drinks and then start talking to a few girls. One of which is so small it makes Kneale Diamond a basketball player in comparison.

Feeling a bit rough the following morning, I head downstairs for a nuclear hot breakfast. I immediately bump into some Swedish guys I know and then sit down opposite one of the course managers I used to work with almost ten years prior. Per and I catch up and plan to meet a little later when I am not so dead.

The day is spent on or around the show stand meeting with customers and colleagues alike. It is busy and very well organised. My diary for the few days is booked full and with so many people to meet just for a chat, time goes by quickly.

The evening was to be another group affair; with this time, the UK sales team inviting customers to join us. I too had several distributors and customers from Europe joining us.

We had booked out an entire restaurant for this. The place served fish and chips. It is a nice place, and I can guess on a typical day the ambience would be calm and the food excellent. This night I am afraid that it was so loud it was hard to hear. The food is well organised and the beer cold.

It was to be an early bed for me as two nights is too much in Harrogate. I know I sound old, but I had booked meetings the following day that started from 9 am until 5 pm. One must be sensible if I want to succeed in my business area and this being the start of the second year it is important.

It is the final day at the show for me. With all my meetings completed I was to meet everyone in our lobby bar before the Scandinavian dinner we had arranged together with a large chemical company. This venue was around the corner from the hotel and the tables were fewer than the previous night this hopefully meant that the noise level was much less. At least this time one could hear the person next to you. I was feeling rubbish and that maybe I was coming down with something. Towards the end of the meal I started to feel light-headed and hot. Still, I ploughed through the enjoyable Italian meal, but as the bill came, I felt like real crap and like a colleague earlier, I had to make a direct line for bed.

Having a good rest and terribly hot breakfast I checked out. Another director of our company gave me a ride back to Manchester airport for my long flight via Oslo home.

At the airport I meet up with a few of my Norwegian customers, so we have a light lunch. The flight was uneventful as I slept most of it still not feeling at my best.

It was good to get back home for a few weeks break before the long line of travel would start again. Prague being the first trip on the list.

35. Prague February 2020

The trip to Prague this time was to attend the Czech Greenkeepers conference set in the University just on the outskirts of the city. My flight over was easy enough and arriving at the airport, I decide to try out the public transport to the town for a change. I usually either drive myself or have our distributor pick me up so opting for public transportation would give me more of a feeling of being adventurous.

The bus is comfortable enough and costs very little money. It drops us at an underground station, and I follow other passengers down into the station. I buy a ticket from the ticket machine that I think covers the journey and then find on the map the closest station to the city centre square where the U Prince Hotel is situated.

I had booked the U Prince hotel as I was late in getting the onsite booking near the conference location. Anyway, I preferred the city for the ease of getting around on foot in the evenings. Prague is an epic city for evening nightlife, and I love to wander in its small streets as you now know.

Coming out of the underground, the weather has changed for the worse. There is now a blizzard outside with heavy sideways-falling snow. It is only about 3 degrees, but with the wind, it feels much colder. I watch as people struggle to see walking down the street with the snow falling in their faces. Amusingly there were a surprising number of people trying to put up umbrellas.

I wait for a bit and have a smoke. Watching the city getting covered in clean white fresh snow is wonderful. It feels soft and calm. The weather eases off, and I take the opportunity to roll my bag down the street. The snow now is collecting on my bag, and I start to plough the snow behind me, leaving a clear path for fellow pedestrians behind me.

Arriving at the hotel check-in, a man escorts me to my room. He opens it and places my now wet bag near the door. He shows me the facilities, and I am very impressed. I have a huge double bed covered in pillows. A desk lies in the corner next to a fully stocked bar. My view is of the stairs to the rooftop terrace, but I don't care as I get my first glance of the bathroom. It is adorned with fluffy white towels, and there is a separate shower and bath. Standing next to the tub is a wooden character holding up a tray of soaps and other items. It looked a little politically incorrect as he was of African descent. Some colonial statue from times past.

Thanking the man he left and I got to unpack and change for the evening. I was to meet up with Kneale Diamond and a guy called Henrik in the bar in the basement of the U Prince. *The Black Angels* Bar is decorated beautifully and is very cosy. It has a 1920's feel and is well known for its cocktails and music.

I walk into the body of the bar and get my phone out to take a photo of the enormous Angel hanging from the ceiling. I am immediately told that I am not allowed to do this by a rude waitress. I do as I am told and walk around. She must have thought I was an idiot tourist from the street. I walk around and she eyes me distastefully. I walk up to the bar, sit down and order a beer.

The guys arrive, and we have a discussion about the conference and what we were to expect. We had not received a vast amount of information and were a little confused as to the plans.

After a simple meal, we plan to meet at the hotel where both Henrik and Kneale Diamond are staying. I was going to take an Uber taxi to them a little before so that we could walk to the registration together.

I was quite pleased the evening was early as I wanted to enjoy my room. Taking a final glass of wine, I settled down on my sofa to watch a program on my iPad.

At about 3 am I wake up on the sofa and move myself to the cold yet fresh and tightly made bed and have an excellent sleep for the rest of the night.

My Uber dropped me off at the hotel near the University at 8 am. Immediately I meet with a few greenkeepers I know. We walk over to the University and try to locate the seminar room that is allocated to our conference room. It is quite a big university, and I am afraid it made me feel old. We were lost and it did look like we were never going to get out of the place.

Finally, we spot a fellow attendee and walk with him since he knew what he was doing. We register, grab a coffee and mingle with the greenkeepers, groundsmen and trade representatives.

The room is big, with a fantastic project car from the engineering department. We are ushered into the lecture dome for the morning seminar. We all sit like students with the speakers looking up towards us. The conference had brought an international array of attendees, so there were both English and Czech speakers.

At the lunch break, we make our way over to the university canteen. The queue is horrendous. Kneale Diamond and I decide to take lunch outside somewhere quiet and have an excellent deep-fried cheese. A fantastic Czech speciality probably developed to absorb the alcohol content in the stomach.

The afternoon proceeds as the morning with speakers and questions: mingling and minor meetings held in the breaks. I had suggested that we do something cultural in the early evening. There was to be a disco of sorts and massive amounts of beer to celebrate the closing of the conference. Not wishing to do this a few of my customers suggested we have a few beers in the city instead.

But first the cultural bit. A museum that I have wanted to visit for a while now is the Museum of Communism. One of my customers, Jordan, is married to a Bulgarian. She has often mentioned what it was like under communist rule. And since The Czech Rep was also under the same type of control until relatively recently, it was interesting to see how life was.

The museum is very well set out, in a very easy to follow manner through different aspects of life under communism. I would suggest anyone wishing to see how life can change in a few decades you should go. We spend a good hour in there walking around and discovering how tough it must have been to be controlled, monitored and sometimes tortured.

We had suggested to another customer of mine, Ben that he join us but he was more interested in a beer or two so the plan was that he find a bar/restaurant and we would meet him there when we finished in the museum.

Our souls and mind filled with culture and images of how life has changed Jordan, Kneale Diamond, and myself walk over to find Ben. He had given us some vague directions to the bar, and eventually, we see it and him with a table full of beer. We immediately order some food and settle down to talk about our visit to Ben, mainly to wind him up a bit.

Dinner finished we head to another new bar for me—*Hemingways* bar. We order some strange cocktails and chat about grass and bunkers for the rest of the evening.

My flight back to Sweden was to be via Frankfurt. This was because I was flying Lufthansa, and it was the cheapest option. I don't mind Frankfurt, and I certainly enjoy flying Lufthansa. On this occasion, however, I had my first ever real issue with airline food. I know I write about little boxes of horribleness on SAS or the useless lack of facilities on BA, but this time I had an issue with Lufthansa's sandwich. I am not joking, but I bit into it and discover that I bit into a piece of metal! An actual piece of metal! Not being American and wanting to take Lufthansa for all their money I kindly told the stewardess and showed her the offending metal shard. She took it and said she needed to write a report. I waited for a free bottle of wine, or even a document to agree that this had happened. Maybe even some extra points for the mishap but nothing. And still to this day I wait.

On my way back home I pondered the trip. I also noted that it was the only time I had been to Prague and not walked over the Charles Bridge.

Next week I shall be off to the UK with children. What I mean is I shall only be flying with two of my children as they stay for a week with friends while I pass on to Dublin and Galway for a European Congress of Greenkeeper Associations. I look forward to a Guinness very much.

36. Ireland February 2020

It is Monday morning, and Lina drops my eldest two children and I off at the local train station. The beginning of a week-long trip for us all. Both of the kids were staying at different friends houses on the South coast of the UK. I would accompany them to the village where we used to live, and then they would be picked up by their friends. I would meet them again on Friday at Gatwick airport.

Our flight was comfortable and smooth. We arrived at Gatwick and took our train to Bosham. With the kids gone, I was left to meet with my brother for a pie and pint in the local pub.

My Ryanair flight to Dublin was the first time in a long while I had flown with them. I am not a fan of their planes and service, but it was the only way this trip would work in the time frame I wanted. I was to fly to Dublin early and then drive to Galway for the conference. I had not been to Galway before and was looking forward to seeing more of Ireland other than Dublin. Our venue was close to the city centre with trips out to golf courses for parts of the conference.

At Gatwick, I am stopped for a proper bag search at security. This does not happen much to me, but I had a bag of metal whistles I had forgotten to take out of my flight bag. With everything cleared, I head towards the *Grain Store* for a hearty breakfast.

After my fill and a quick look in the bookshop, I board the yellow monster for the short but cramped flight to Dublin. The guy sitting next to me had had a few more breakfasts and was struggling with the seat buckle. He had not loosened it and had still managed to fasten it in. I did not want him to die of lack of oxygen so I unbuckled it for him and showed him how to make it fit him better. He thanked me and took out his iPad and watched a Japanese children's movie for the duration of the flight.

My hire car was a Golf. I love these cars. We have one at home. I believe that they are very reliable and sturdy cars. And excellent to drive too. This one was not, however. It started with an engine warning light which I was told not to worry about. The drive to Galway is a good few hours on a long and frankly dull road. I hit a little traffic arriving into Galway and head straight for the hotel. I wanted a shower and a Guinness.

On check-in, I discover that the swimming pool and gym were open and they looked very enticing. Why not. I had brought my training gear, so I head immediately down to get a good sweat on before that first pint of Irish Guinness.

On my way out of the gym, I see Lee. He was checking in, so we make arrangements for the bar. All of the guys in our Turf Travels group were to attend so I was sure it would be a good conversation and probably a few too many drinks.

The reception dinner was simple but very nice. It was great to meet customers from all over Europe. We mingled and chatted for hours. It is at this stage when you know it is a bad idea to head into town for a few more.

A few of us did, and at one stage, I remember being at an icy house party with Lee and a few others. Some were arguing about a taxi fare, and so I thought I would step in. I took the cab covered the fare with a little extra for the "problem" and left the others there.

The second day was to be held at the Galway Bay Hotel conference centre. It is a large room in the basement of the hotel we are staying. The morning was to be various speeches on products and developments in the industry with the afternoon set aside for what would be a type of speed dating. Each company "Sponsor" would have a table where the delegates would listen to five minutes of sales talk before moving on to the next table.

This turned out to be both brilliant and extremely tiring at the same time. We deserved a beer after this. I almost lost my voice completely. After the speed dating, we all piled into the lobby bar and then had a few more discussions with customers and clients.

The dinner was set in the city. The restaurant, which I forget the name of as usual, had a salsa type of theme. It was brilliant, and I do kick myself for not remembering it. As soon as the dinner ended, there was a bit of a split up. Some people went back to the hotel and others; I included, fancied a pint in the bar down the road. We wanted to listen to live music and enjoy the Irish hospitality a little longer.

It was to be another late night. At one point one of our crowd, name to be exempt but it starts with a Jim, lost his coat with the only remaining coat left in the bar being similar but from Dorothy Perkins. He left it.

The next morning the weather had got worse. There was some storm heading our way, but to me, it looked like it had arrived. It wasn't very pleasant. We were to have an afternoon of panel discussions and speeches at a golf club on the other side of the Galway Bay. The bus that was to take us there was late, so I suggested that I could drive. It was not far, and that way if I wanted to leave a little earlier I could. I took a few of the guys with me, and we started up the Golf. It did not sound right. It was like starting a car from the 1970s. It took a while, and then it was fine. Occasionally losing power but it was a Golf so it would work.

After the speeches and in particular an inspirational panel discussion by five "Women in Golf", we returned the hotel. The last night was to be a pub dinner in the lobby bar. This bar had served us well this week but having almost 100 delegates pile in at the same time, all wanting drinks was a bit too much for the lone barman. I ordered a wine and almost spat it out it was so bad. As the barman saw this, he gave me a beer instead.

I had planned not being up later than 10 pm. I had an early day driving the broken Golf back to Dublin before catching my flight to meet the kids at Gatwick. I was right to my word ish and left the rest of the guys there to enjoy.

Waking up at 4 am to check out I bump into a bunch of Turf Travellers sitting in the lobby. They had just come in! I say my goodbyes and leave in the spluttering Golf.

I was a little worried about the weather and the flight. The rain and wind had not stopped all night, and the drive was treacherous. In the end, I made it with good time in hand, explained the issues with the car and had a surprisingly smooth flight back to the London.

On meeting my children, we catch up and have time to buy some things before our flight to Stockholm. The seat behind me had a very young child, and it was repeatedly kicking me for half the flight. My daughter found this very funny. But then the child was moved behind her, so she stopped laughing.

The next week was supposed to be Italy, and the My Plant and Garden show in Milan. Over the weekend the situation in Italy with COVID had gotten very much worse, and it was to be cancelled last second. This was to be the beginning of the end of the world of my travels.

37. Norway March 2020

After the coronavirus outbreak in Italy had caused the cancellation of the My Plant and Garden show, I have spent the past week working from home and watching how the situation across Europe developed. It does not look good.

I am reluctant to book too far ahead now because of the spread of the virus. There are two trips left on my reserved list, Norway and Iceland. Both countries had no travel restrictions at the time of writing, and I prepared myself for the overland trip to Norway.

Lina drops me off at the train station in Degerfors where I would take the high-speed train to Karlstad and then the bus to Oslo City. As you have read, this is a trip I have done before. This time, however, there were signs of distance amongst passengers. If you coughed, you are looked at as if you have the Plague and people edge away trying to breathe in from another direction.

On the bus sat a man playing a child's game with the sound on. I don't know how anyone can do this without caring for fellow passengers. Even with my headphones, I could still hear the faint beeping sound.

I put my audiobook on a bit louder and tried to ignore the guy. At the border into Norway we are directed into a hanger. I have crossed the border between Seden and Norway many times and have never been stopped. And remember this is a European Union to non-European border. The Scandinavians had a cross border deal well before the EU was invented. There are a few other cars in there, and customs officials and their dogs were searching inside them. A man came on to our bus, and we had to show our identification cards or passports. He asked where we were from and asked what we were doing in Norway. All was fine. Then another customs officer came on with the cutest of dogs. She walked the dog down while it jumped up and smelled each passenger. A third man came on board, and while the dog was jumping and smelling the luggage in the hold, we are asked how much tobacco and alcohol we all had in our bags. This was very interesting. The amount of whisky and wine being brought into Norway on this bus was enough to have a month-long party. If we broke down in the middle of nowhere we would be fine.

The first customs official came back onto the bus holding up a bag asking who's it was. The irritating man on the child's game owned up after a while and then was asked to show all his luggage.

It was hard to see through the doors to the outside. Both hold doors were up covering the window, but between the gaps of the doors was a slither of sightline. The passenger sitting next to me started to giggle. I looked at him, and he suggested I look. The guy taken off of our bus had his bag stuffed full of cigarettes, two pairs of underwear and nothing else. The contents now spread across the inspection table. I smiled and sat back and waited.

It turned out we did not have to wait long as the driver of our bus is informed by one of the customs officials that we could go, leaving the cigarette guy there to explain himself.

On arrival into Oslo, I find my first meeting is unfortunately cancelled. I, therefore, pick up my hire car and head directly for call number two on my list. After a good discussion with Duncan, John and Luna the dog I make my way to the out of town hotel I had booked to be close to the following days first call. I am to meet with Duncan again for dinner, together with Eoin, an Irishman at the course I was to visit the next morning.

My arrival at the Moxy Hotel in Oslo was not grand. To be honest, it was not easy to locate the car parking. Or the entrance to the hotel. I followed signs for what looked like the entrance, but it took me to the back of what looked like an exhibition hall. It is an exhibition hall, and the hotel is an annexe of it. Parking finally I rolled my bag through the snow to the entrance. Inside the lobby, the lighting is quite mesmerising. It changes slowly and feels out of place somehow.

I check-in and after a short hiccup with my booking, I am offered my room key. The room is small yet cosy. I have a double bed, a view of a car park, and a small shower/bathroom. I turn on the lights and my room glowed. I am disappointed that the room does not have a desk. I had several emails to respond to, and it is not that easy doing this with an iPad and separate keyboard on the bed. I move to the lobby bar/cafe/restaurant/games room/meeting point and sit down with a large coffee and complete my work.

Having showered and changed, I go back to the confused room of many things to meet Eoin and Duncan. We order some food, and the waiter is baffled with our accents. Not typical for a Norwegian as they are brilliant at English. We hope we receive what we order.

After our incredibly expensive burgers and four portions of fries, we have a final drink before parting. The room is still packed when we are walking out. I asked a woman at the bar what was going on. She informs me that the hotel is fully booked with delegates for an energy expo in the exhibition hall. I thought it wise not to mingle and went to sleep.

My sleep is interrupted so many times by people knocking into the walls and doors of the corridor. I lay there amazed how these guys could get so drunk. The drinks in this place were unbelievably expensive. Maybe they had massive expense accounts.

I get up at 6 am and go down in the hunt for coffee and something to eat. I checked out on my way and hoped that the next hotel closer to the city waterfront would be quieter.

After my day's visits, I get to my Thorn hotel in the Oslo fjord. I find I am gutted to discover that this was in dire need of renovation. There was evidence that this was in process, but I am booked in the cheap room at the back. My room does have a desk, and I use it to catch up on a bit of work. The hotel did have a swimming pool, and I toyed with the idea of a swim, but after looking at the green monster, I decided not to. The bar and restaraunt opened at 6 pm. I am there for the moment it opened. I am so tired I did not care for anything, just food and bed. The choice was fish or burger. I choose the burger. It was good, but I should have had the fish. Hardly keeping awake I order the bill and am in bed at 8 pm.

After a wonderful dream free deep sleep I awake alive a ready for the long day ahead and driving through the Oslo fjords, I had a new golf course to visit that a greenkeeper that was a customer of mine at another club, had moved to. I also had two other courses to see in the area.

With the roads very slippery, I finally make it around and then back into Oslo city for my last hotel night of the week. The Scandic Vulcan is a good spot. One of my favourite as it is walking distance to the city without being in it, but far enough out to be cheap. It boasts expensive parking but surrounded by great restaurants and the "*Mathallen*", or "food hall", which host bars and a selection of cool food eateries. I walk around the food hall and buy some dried whale and some Norwegian oak-aged cheese.

I often go to *Bar Social* when I am here. A restaurant where you have tapas-style food at a reasonable price, good wine and an amiable atmosphere and great staff.

I order a Lebanese house wine to go with some chilli crab taco and grilled cabbage in a brilliant sauce covered in nuts, and it is all sublime.

During dinner, the purchase of my whale had been reversed on my debit card. So happy days. I got a free whale. Well, a little bit of one anyway. After putting these in the boot of the car to keep cool, I relax with a movie and hot chocolate.

Over breakfast, I discover that my meeting in Hemsedal is cancelled. Being Thursday, it meant that I could fit one of my Friday meetings in and have less time stress on my travel day home.

The drive to Honefoss is always breathtaking, and I have written about this before. The road meanders through the sides of the fjord until it spits you out with a massive view over the water and islands that sit within it. At this time of year, the snow sits softly on the trees. The roads are icy but freshly ploughed. As I get to the bridge over to the golf Island of Tyrifjord, I find the farmer ploughing the snow from it. I am not sure my little hire car would have managed without it. I meet with Ian, the course manager there and his assistant Nick. We discuss the course and all of our products for the year. We discuss the virus situation also. There is a discussion on how life would be like if it spread over the whole of Europe and if it would affect my work. I could not imagine it happening as how would that work. All borders closed. Never. We laugh over the situation of Brexit and how the Boris would probably want a full lockdown of borders permanently.

We move on, and I follow Ian back to his house to see the family and have a wonderful home-cooked meal made by his wife. As I am staying there, we are to have one of our whisky evenings too with our friends PG and Rob, the Dutchman.

The last day of my trip to Norway takes me back to the outskirts of the city to a golf course at a school. I meet with Gavin, and we go through the usual sales motions.

Leaving him, I managed to book an earlier bus and train connection back home. I ditched the hire car at the central train station and walked over the bridge to the bus station. I caught up with the news that Austria and a few other countries were now getting more infections. It was increasing fast, and various European countries were recording their first victims. It was not good news. I had only one more trip left on my booking list, and I wanted to get it done before things get really out of hand. I had already received an email from the office stating that I should not book anything too far in advance and that anything I had booked might have to be rescheduled for a few months in the future.

The bus ride was comfortable and smooth, with no border issues. And with only a short wait I boarded the train in Karlstad for the short trip back home, to my waiting wife. It was very strange to have dinner on a Friday night at home with the family for a change, but it was so lovely at the same time. I was only to be home for the Saturday as I had to stay overnight on Sunday to get the first flight out of Stockholm to Oslo for my connection to Reykjavik. A week in Iceland with an epic road trip to the northern part.

38. Iceland March 2020

I pushed the day as long as possible to be with the family, which meant that I would get in late to my hotel and hit the bed immediately to get the most sleep I could. The morning arrives far too quickly, and I am up at 5 am ready and on my way on the fast train to the airport.

The flight connection at Oslo was brief and stress-free as I walked off of one plane I turned left and got in line at the next gate onto and onto the plane to Reykjavik.

Iceland at this time of the year is best described and changeable. The wind was harsh and strong, bitterly battering everything in sight, including my face.

I walk out of the terminal and found my Polo hire car. After removing ice crystals and inch thick, I drive to the first club on my visit list for the day.

The little Polo wobbled about the road in the wind. It did not feel super safe at all. The roads were icy, but the winter tyres held me vaguely straight. There is little snow, probably because it had no chance to land, it is blown off back into the Ocean.

The trip over was noticeably different. People were starting to keep distance, and a few announcements in the airports requested people to keep a distance from each other as well as keeping an eye over their bags. This Coronavirus was beginning to irritate plans of any travel across borders. Over the weekend Europe had certainly started to close borders or cancel flights with refunds or postponements. But it was mostly in the South of Europe, and although a few cases were popping up in Scandinavia, it felt that everything was under control.

After my visits were completed, I had a frozen face. All I wanted to do was find the hotel, check-in and defrost in the shower. The Agronomist was also arriving for his first visit to Iceland. We were both to be presenting at the Icelandic conference the next day. I had not seen the Agronomist since he left our company to work more with the football side of life. It would be great to catch up with him and also know how the new role was going.

Defrosted, I met with the Agronomist, and we had dinner together over a few beers. We met with some greenkeepers I knew and had a few more and got to bed quite late.

We arrive for the seminar at 10 am. The venue is the National Stadium, A fantastic looking place and the first time I had ever seen a warm air cover over a football pitch. We, unfortunately, were told to go away and come back at lunchtime as the Icelandic's had some meeting that did not include trade. We decide to drive over to see a customer of mine and also have a look at the furthest most point of the coastline of Reykjavik.

We visited an English guy who had taken over as course manager for a club I knew. The Agronomist knew him years ago while working in Norway. It was time for a catch-up. We had a walk around the course and went upstairs to his indoor putting room. Very strange to have this facility, but if you think about it makes perfect sense to have as much indoor as possible in Iceland. And putting was something you could not do today in this wind.

We enjoyed a vegetable soup in the clubhouse and discussed the history of the club. After this delicious and warming lunch, we needed to head back to the Stadium to present our presentations.

The presentation went well. It was different to have people in front of you set between a laptop screen with a delegate attending on Skype. He is located in the far north of Iceland in Akureyri, at the club I would visit the following day. A good six-hour drive through volcanic mountains and high coast roads. For him, it was regular use of the excellent internet that is set up in Iceland. I thought that it might be one day how us sales guys would work, but I still think that meeting in person is so essential. Someone would surely take up the environmental impact of us flying around. But I only cover Europe, so I should not be affected, I thought.

After the presentations of the afternoon were done we mingled with the delegates and they brought out the beer for a farewell cheer. I like this way of ending a meeting.

I suggested to the Agronomist that he sees one of the most breath-taking golf courses I have ever seen. Klettar golf course is different in many ways. It is not 18 holes for a start. The idea is that why not 15 holes? Well, who can argue with that? The course has a collection of the most outstanding golf holes ever, in my opinion. Most of the holes are right on the ocean edge. The wind is madness, and the sand is black. The greens sometimes get sprayed with rock from the waves and occasionally fish.

I drove us there, and we walked around for a bit, drove around for a little bit more and the Agronomist agreed that it was up there in his top 5 clubs in the world that he had visited.

Back in town, I had booked the restaurant. We were to be a few guys and to make it cheap, and the best idea was to go for a tapas-style table buffet of local dishes.

Now I can't remember the dishes in complete detail but the animals that were involved in their construction were; Lamb, Chicken,

Whale, Pig, Kangaroo, Scallop, Beef, Puffin, Pork, and Duck.

I am not sure how the Kangaroo became part of the "local dishes", but it may have just looked like a good idea at the time.

I do remember that I preferred the puffin to the chicken. The food is excellent and memorable, if not only for the collection of animals that were consumed.

I went to bed not so much full, but satisfied and weirdly guilty of the number of animals I had eaten in just one meal, even if the dishes were minimal.

The Agronomist was to leave for the UK, and I was to drive to Akureyri. At breakfast, I informed the Agronomist that I was to pass by and visit an English guy, Darren. He could join me in his car and then we could split from there. He agreed, and we drove to the club in thick snow and more wind.

On our arrival, we sat down and had a coffee together. The guys looked at my hire car just laughed at my plan to drive up to Akureyri. They showed me the road on the computer. The only country I the world I know that has cameras at numerous points on the road so you could see how bad it was. As I have said before, here the weather changes in a blink of an eye. And the road 1 is often closed due to lousy weather. They said it would be impossible to get to Akureyri and I should cancel or fly there. I agreed. I would cancel. I am not completely convinced a flight would be the best for safety or my expense account.

The roads looked passable with a 4X4, and I have to say that I would think twice about doing it in my own Land Rover Defender. The mechanic had a Defender with enormous tyres that could be inflated and deflated without getting out. It also had Marine Satellite Navigation for reasons unknown to me. It is prepared for the Arctic, not like my little Polo hire car.

In the car park, I said goodbye to the Agronomist and made the call to Steindor in Akureyri. He agreed that it would be foolish even to try, and with more bad weather to come, we would keep in touch via the internet.

I had next to rebook myself into the same Hotel Kletter as I had been for the first part of the week. I would lose one night in the hotel I had in Akureyri so needed one night back in Reykjavik.

On arrival, I told the reception that they need not give me a new room. I could have the one I had vacated this same morning. They agreed and said to me that I had to wait for room booking app to come through with the booking reference. The receptionist told me to drop my bag into the luggage room two floors down, and then I could wait.

On my return to the front desk, my booking had come in, so I checked back in, then retrieved my bag from its five-minute stay in an underground cupboard. I went to my room to plan the two days I now had free.

I put in orders from the previous week and got in touch with a few of the guys around Reykjavík to see if they could see me. Thankfully I filled my first day with a visit to a golf course set in a lava field. It is again, extraordinary. I had been here before and have written about it. It is the one that was a zoo.

Getting back to my hotel, I decide that another soup would be a great idea. Again I have been and written about this place before. It is the place that serves the soup in a massive bread roll. For me it a place I will return again and again.

I had my soup and then popped into the bar that always has been a place I meet new people. And it did not disappoint. I met a guy from Zanzibar and a girl who was Russian banker living in Nice. We had a few drinks, and I left. The weather outside was properly arctic.

I was due to visit a football club in the city first thing in the morning, and I was so happy it could be arranged so late.

After the meeting, I had to move hotel. It was only a few hundred meters from the Kletter but much much worse. It is the sort of hotel that doesn't like giving you the room until the designated check-in time, 3 pm and not a moment earlier saying the room was not ready. I sat in the lobby bar with a coffee and waited while catching up on emails. I don't believe that the room is not prepared, how can all the rooms be unready until 3 minutes to 3 in the afternoon. Maybe gusts in the past have stolen all the towels and coffee making facilities so now you get only the smallest amount of time in the room.

As I wait, I notice that the many guests are wearing masks and that we are only allowed to be in the lobby bar for 15 minutes or a maximum number of people. The fact that it was sideways snow falling outside I could not again understand why we're not checked into the rooms. The smell of hand sanitiser was wafting through the room. I quite like the bouquet personally, but it does give a sense of dentist waiting room.

Eventually, I am given my key and told that people in the same room could only use the elevator. My room is on the third floor, so I wait for two other groups to go up before me, even though a week ago we would all be in there together.

The room is also rubbish and adorned with signs of many things that you can be charged for if you don't go by the rules. The bed was noisy and uncomfortable and small. The balcony door was inoperable, and the room was cold. The sideways snow had stopped, and the sun was out. It looked like a perfect walking evening. I went to the bathroom. The shower has hot sulphur smelling water that was nice to shower in—the only upside of the room.

After dressing, I catch up on some up on emails and without noticing the weather went from bliss blue sky to blizzard. The visibility was about the edge of my balcony. I was so thankful I had not made it up to Akureyri.

The evening plan was that I have dinner alone, and then I was to meet up with a group of Greenkeepers for a few drinks. They had told me that I should try to go to two different Icelandic bars and then we would meet in the Scottish one. I thought this was an adequate plan, so I went out to *Bastard Brew Pub* for dinner. Bastard is very well priced and would recommend it. The beer they make themselves and the food is international pub grub and good.

Next place I am told to visit is simply translated as the Old Danish bar. It is one of the oldest in town, and I do not enjoy it as much. It is full of very drunk locals, and I stood out like a sore thumb. A very different scene and I left as soon as I finished a beer.

I head to meet the greenkeepers in the Scottish *Brew Dog* bar. I like *Brew Dog* beer and drink it whenever I am in the mood for beer. I like their type of beer. We had an enjoyable evening of them filling me in on the industry in Iceland, and I have to say that this was probably the most informative evening with them. It is so lovely to relax with a bunch of guys, now customers only having met three times before and talk bollox in a pub. This is how all good business relationships start, I think, and probably why meeting people in person is so vital in any sales role. It is the chemistry of the relationship that builds trust and friendship.

I awake to discover that my flight from Copenhagen to Stockholm has been cancelled. And the flight to Copenhagen from Reykjavik is delayed. Denmark had closed its borders. It is now the top priority to get to Copenhagen. From there, I could at least go overland home. Norway was following suit, and it looked like Europe was closing different parts every hour.

At the airport, I get through to the departure lounge, pick up a lucky troll creature for my shelf of shit and order a tuna and avocado sandwich which was different but I felt like trying it. Usually, I would think this combination would not have worked, but I stand here saying try it. It is excellent.

Thankfully the flight to Copenhagen is only delayed due to the weather, and we take off only 40 minutes late. I don't care, I am airborne and on my way to Denmark. I thought that I would relax and have a nice coffee.

Just after we get to cruising altitude and the steward and flight attendants are released to serve the passengers. We are informed by the captain that due to the health of our passenger's drinks would not be served. Also, the toilet at the front of the cabin would be for flight staff only. We all had to use the toilets in the rear of the plane.

I sit there slightly irritated that this virus is beginning to give people paranoia. On arrival in Copenhagen, I head to SAS lounge for a wine. I had to wait for the final flight to Stockholm so I may as well complete the work for the prior week over some food and wine in the lounge.

The voices over the tannoy continue to explain that we need to keep apart from each other. There are mask-wearing people everywhere, and the smell of hand sanitiser fills the air. On entering the SAS lounge, I read the sign saying I must sanitise my hands before picking anything from the bar.

I sit and watch the news. I look at the BBC, Euro News, and SVT. All are reporting the same. It seems like I would be grounded for a while. Borders are closing, and I absolutely did not want to either get caught in a country when airports were closing or catch this little virus. I would be safest at home.

So this was to be the last flight and indeed trip for a while, everything is cancelled everywhere.

Acknowledgments and Thanks

I would like to thank Carl. This book would never have been possible without him and the company I am so immensely proud to work for.

A big acknowledgement goes out to Turf Travellers everywhere. What we do as sales people is not easy, but what we can do is make it fun.

A special thanks to all my customers all over Europe. You have made the story come alive. Not wanting to name names, you know who you are.

Thanks to all the associations and event organisers in the Turf industry that made the events that these stories come from. If we do not meet then lifelong friendships and binding relationships could never happen and funny little stories would never be told.

A big thanks go to my wife Lina, The designer of this cover!

And finally thanks to my young family for being so amazing. I truly have missed you on all these trips away. You are travellers at heart and I hope you continue to do so in your future life.

Coming soon, my next book…

Follow the Man on the Donkey